I Remember Me
The First 25 Years

FRANK IFIELD

With

Pauline Halford

km
Kempton
MARKS

A Kempton Marks Book

Copyright © Frank Ifield and Pauline Halford 2005

Cover design by Siobhan Smith ©

Frank Ifield and Pauline Halford have asserted the moral right to be identified as the authors of this work.

All rights reserved. No part of this publication may be reproduced, stored in a retrieval system, or transmitted in any form or by any means, electronic, mechanical, photocopy, recording or otherwise, without prior written permission of the copyright owners. Nor can it be circulated in any form of binding or cover other than that in which it is published and without similar condition including this condition being imposed on a subsequent purchaser.

ISBN 0 7552 0501 4

Kempton Marks
40 Castle Street
Hertford SG14 1HR
England

This book is also available in e-book format, details of which are available at www.authorsonline.co.uk

I dedicate this book to my dear mother, my brothers, and to my beloved wife Carole for their love and support through both the good years and the times of adversity.

Acknowledgements

Whilst wishing to thank all those who have also been supportive of me on my universal journey, I pay special homage to my mentors. Those whose extraordinary belief in my abilities, enabled me to grow in order to feel worthy of their faith. Their encouragement helped me to reach for the highest stars and express my soul by giving vent to my passion in life:

My dear departed father Richard J Ifield;
Allan Crawford (Former Manager of Southern Music Australia);
Ron Wills (Recording manager of EMI Australia);
Peter Gormley (My personal manager);
Norrie Paramore (Recording Manager of EMI UK);
Leslie Grade (Grade Organisation - Agency UK);
Wesley Rose (General Manager of Acuff/Rose & Hickory records USA).

HULL LIBRARIES	
HULL CENTRAL LIBRARY	
01115128 3	
Bertrams	15.12.05
782.42164	£10.99
BIO	

Co-author's Note

Many people have contributed their help and expertise to the making of this book and, on behalf of Frank and myself, I thank them all. First and foremost are the members of the Ifield family, especially Frank's mother Muriel who has provided a host of memories from Frank's early days. Practical help has been freely and generously given by, amongst others, Bob Howe, Colin Ifield, Cosy Dixon and Mary Payne, while technical assistance in the production of the book has come from Dione Coombe, Wendy Lake, Siobhan Smith who designed the jacket and publisher Richard Fitt of Authors OnLine Ltd.

Finally, I would like to add my personal thanks to Frank for providing me with the unique opportunity of working with him on writing his life story. Little did I realise, when we started, that Frank has crammed so much into his life that it will take two books to do it justice. We hope you, the reader, will enjoy this, the first volume, and will look forward with anticipation to its sequel.

Pauline Halford

Preface

This biographic book depicts my first 25 years; the full story has taken more than a decade to write and has turned out far too large for one volume. Yet even this first part might not have materialised at all had it not been for my friend and musical director Bob Howe. Bob loved to hear 'behind the scenes' stories and urged me to write them down as the story of my life. Non-stop touring around the world made my life too hectic back then to attempt such a mind-boggling project. Then fate intervened and during an enforced recuperation following my hospitalisation in Australia, my brother Colin took upon himself an important role as 'Dr Fix-it'. He believed, quite rightly, that jotting down my memoirs, while teaching me to use a computer, would also prove therapeutic for my grey-matter; the therapy worked and although it was done purely for that reason, it nevertheless spawned the book's humble beginnings.

Enter Pauline Halford (herself a professional author). She made a timely approach from England with a desire to write a biography about me, and I felt comfortable that we could achieve it together, despite the tyranny of the distance between us.

We have tried to faithfully sketch in the background of my formative years, coloured by my own emotional feelings and as seen through my eyes at the age I was at the time. My beloved home countries of Britain and Australia may well have changed much with the passage of time, yet my love and pride in them both has remained constant.

Now, having entered the 21st century, my wife Carole and I have been further blessed in the role of grandparents to a bright-eyed, eager-to-learn young lad by the name of Jack. So I feel it may be good for us all to reflect upon our yesterdays, if only to pass on for perpetuity the good things we have been privileged to learn from our experiences. By adhering to the positives in our individual lives, I hope we all might find inspiration together, allowing us to face the uncertain world of tomorrow with strength, greeting a brand new unwritten chapter of life as a positive challenge.

Frank Ifield

PROLOGUE

I left my homeland Australia,
In search of the bright lights of fame;
But I realise now what I miss most of all,
When I hear that 'Waltzing Matilda' again:
I've seen lots of places and cities – Too many to mention by name,
From the U.S. of A – Right across the U.K.
They play, that Waltzing Matilda Again.

[Play Waltzing Matilda Again]

We were all stripped down to our underpants - roadies, musicians and artists alike. The year was 1986 and we were on a concert tour of Western Australia, a test of endurance we had nicknamed the 'Agent's Revenge'. Our conveyance was a charabanc, a clapped out relic upon which one could faintly make out the word 'Pioneer' emblazoned on its faded livery. Its only claim to modernisation was an air-conditioning unit I'm certain was there just for show. It coughed and protested its way through some of the most inhospitable territory of the barren red outback of Australia, whose sterile skies mocked us as we melted away in the incredible heat; a temperature so oppressive that Dante's 'Inferno' would seem like paradise in comparison. Nobody spoke for hours. We just stared motionless, as any unnecessary movement would only create more heat, and we had already depleted the amber nectar needed to replenish the loss of vital body fluids.

Narrowing my eyes against the glare, I caught sight of Bob Howe - my friend, musical arranger, bandleader and guitarist, all rolled into one. Bob, who was squinting back at me, managed a sentence: "What in the hell are we doing here Frank?" he gasped.

On a deep intake of hot air, I offered "I dunno Bob. I was thinking that maybe I'd passed into purgatory where, for my sins, I'm destined to suffer this gruelling tour with you guys for all eternity."

"Yeah, I can identify with that," nodded Bob.

Conversation lapsed. Time slid tortuously towards the wide horizon. From beyond the red haze of my consciousness, Bob was speaking again.

"It's a shame you haven't written your life story."

I darted a quizzical look at him. What in blazes was he on about?

"You know," he continued, "so people could learn the unadorned truth behind the so-called 'glamour' of showbiz."

I Remember Me

I gave a grunt as we looked around the bus crammed with oozing bodies. Somewhere behind, someone farted, while another was snoring loudly. Yes, Bob was right, there *was* a distinct lack of glamour here.

"Come on," he badgered, "how about starting it now?" It must have been a formidable task for him to drag *any* stories out of me, but he allowed no surrender, and I suppose it passed the time. Eventually, I'd had enough.

"Give it a break, Bob," I pleaded. "My brain's on the boil, and I'm far too hot and weary for all this. Anyhow, my eyes are meant for looking forward, not back. To me, the past is an already written chapter."

"If that be the case," he declared, "it shouldn't take long to rewrite it."

Point taken Bob, I thought. I'd had some experience in writing the sleeve notes for LP records and, more recently, I had tried my hand as a regular columnist, writing for a show-business magazine. My prowess for one-finger typing was certainly improving, but did that qualify me for the mammoth undertaking of writing the story of my life? Even if I tried, just where would I begin?

I closed my eyes in thought. The monotonous drumming of the wheels droned on and I felt myself drifting away, slipping across the dimensions of time to where the past lay shrouded in a deep and distant dream...

- 1 -
THE MORNING OF MY LIFE

I was an awkward cuss from the start. Born a Tuesday's child, I was meant to be full of grace, yet Mum's recollection is of an event far from graceful. I battled hard, even breaching in the struggle, and from my very first intake of breath gave vent to a vocal range to rival the great Pavorotti. So desperate was I to arrive on the day of St Andrew, patron saint of my Scottish forbears and the birthday of the renowned statesman, Sir Winston Churchill, that when it came to a clash of wills, I was determined to have my way. That, they say, is the predisposition of all ambitious archers born under the fiery sign of Sagittarius.

According to the records, the Ifield family was situated at 98 Evenlode Crescent, Radford, Coventry West, on November 30th 1937 when I, Francis Edward, made my materialisation. However, before the patter of my tiny feet could make any impression on the streets of Coventry, I was swept up and moved to No.1, Wherretts Well Lane, Solihull. This may well have been the first manifestation of those influences that were to give my restless soul its wanderlust.

I was not yet two years old when along came 1939 with its declaration of World War Two. The buzzwords were 'War Effort', and we were directed to blacken all our windows during the hours of darkness. To me, this seemed an all-out attempt to prevent people from peering in and disturbing my new kid brother, William Robert, who kicked his way noisily into our clan on May 7th 1941. Yet even his shrill protests were drowned by the bombardment of the blitzes then pounding nightly on Birmingham and Coventry.

In spite of being issued with a Mickey Mouse disguise, which they told me was a gas mask, the enemy still recognised me and continued flinging its bombs - so we upped and left for London. Yet, even here, there was no escape. The culprit, who I discovered was a maniac by the name of Hitler, was still trying to locate me. However, our new home in Ealing Common was cunningly camouflaged within a coppice as if to frustrate the Führer's search. This house boasted a flat roof and our family would venture up there in the evenings to thrill to the sight of brightly coloured tracer bullets shooting through the searchlights into the night sky.

One night as we watched, a British Mosquito fighter plane gave chase to an enemy bomber. In order to make its escape, the bomber jettisoned its load and I was jumping up and down in excitement at the spectacular

I Remember Me

display of bombs hurtling towards me, when suddenly I was yanked away and rushed inside to be shoved, along with the entire family, into the tiny space beneath our staircase – and not a moment too soon.

A mighty eruption blasted my eardrums and our whole house expanded; soot came down the chimney, the back door flew open and black smoke billowed in around us. When the noise subsided, I heard a faint, pathetic meow and as the dust began to settle, the silhouette of Gran's adopted black cat stood trembling in the open doorway. His fur was sticking straight out and his glazed eyes were wide with utter shock. Slowly he lifted and stretched one paw at a time, checking to see it was still there, then sighed with relief to find he was still a fully intact cat.

♪♫♪♫♪

By rights, I should never have been here, caught up with Hitler and his conflict. I belonged 12,000 miles away and had it not been for my father's genius and engineering skill, that's where I would have been.

Both Mum and Dad were Australians, born and bred, but the depression-hit Australia of the 1930's offered neither space nor opportunity for my father to fully develop his creative ideas. So in 1935, my dad, Richard Joseph Ifield, set out in search of an outlet for his inventive abilities. He possessed only the £5 in his pocket and the ambition burning in his soul when he, his nineteen-year-old wife, Hannah Muriel, and baby son, Jim, embarked at Sydney's Woolloomooloo docks for a voyage that would take them half way round the globe, into the unknown.

Times were hard at the start. In order to save a sixpenny bus fare, he'd walk several miles to work at the Riley Motorcar Company of Coventry, where he found his first job. Through diligence, talent and sheer hard work, he soon began to make his mark and took his expanding family with him as he followed his calling around the country. He'd intended to stay for five years but war intervened, so there we were, well and truly stuck in the midst of it.

For Dad, war brought an opportunity he could never have envisaged. Military necessity sparked rapid technological advance and my father was to find himself ideally placed to play his part in it. But for Mum, it was quite a different matter.

The Morning of my Life

I Remember Me

♪♫♪♫♪

A loving memory will always sit comfortably on the mind. Such was the warm and wonderful feeling of closeness I experienced with my mum and the rest of our brood, as we huddled together during the air raids, beneath the protection of a large billiard table that took up most of the space in our lounge.

Cushions and blankets were piled around its sides to shield us against falling debris or flying glass and we would crawl inside, cosy, like in a 'cubby house' or make-believe tent. Within these close confines, supplied with the comfort and warmth of a bottomless flask of tea, I felt safe and secure, while guns boomed, missiles screeched and ominous thuds reverberated all around.

On one such occasion, the stench of smoke was just too close for comfort. In spite of Gran's assurance that she must have left something on the stove, it certainly didn't smell of her cooking to me. The aroma of her pastries, scones and Johnnycakes never failed to make my mouth water. Still, Mum and Gran seemed cool, calm and collected, so I felt there was no need to worry. Even so, we remained in our sanctuary until my father returned home. He burst in, excitedly telling us of all the incendiary bombs littering our road and how the Air Raid Police had defused them. I rushed to take a peek, and there was one by our very own front gate, still smouldering. How lucky we were it didn't bear our number.

Despite the dramatic background of death and destruction, we were told life must go on as normal. Yet what did I, as a child, know of 'normal' life? This was the only existence I knew and it all seemed pretty regular to me. I thought little of the buzz bombs and the blitzkrieg and remained blissfully ignorant of the horrors they wrought. Grown-ups worried over these things, while we kids just got on with having fun. The morning after a raid, we'd venture onto the streets littered with debris, searching for jagged pieces of shiny shrapnel we might sell for pennies, or swap for cigarette-cards and marbles.

It was said that times were tough, with wartime rationing and shortages. However, this wasn't evident to me, nor did it matter much, having to wear hand-me-downs. Quite the contrary. I was proud to be seen in my bigger brothers' cast-offs.

Naturally, I looked up to my elder brothers. First in the pecking order was our Jim, who came blessed with a wonderful shock of curly, almost white hair, a willing smile and a desire to lead by good example. Our John, next in line, was way ahead of the queue when they were handing

The Morning of my Life

out good-looks. He was a regular Rudolph Valentino, tall, dark and handsome. I was third in line and had inherited a few rather strange quirks like my straw-coloured hair, dead straight but for one ridiculous kiss-curl in the middle of my forehead. I also came complete with freckles, of the kind protective mothers passed off as 'sun kisses', and topped off with an over-generously-sized head, somewhat out of proportion to my thin gangling frame. Mum explained that I was still growing, as I stretched onwards and upwards to extend towards the age of five.

My brothers and I were best mates, and although we would often wrestle and call each other names, woe betide the outsider taking the same liberty. John, only sixteen months my senior, was my idol, my best friend and my constant companion. We two were inseparable - playing together, fighting together, in and out of scrapes. I do admit to allowing the green-eyed monster to take me over once, when waiting jealously for his pedal car to be handed down. After all, there was only just over a year between us and he'd had it for such a long time. I confess I would sneak it away, at great risk to my own safety, to use when he wasn't looking.

Overtaken by the green-eyed monster of jealousy, I can't wait to get my hands on brother John's pedal car.

John, meanwhile, had passed the ripe old age of six and, he reckoned, had reached maturity - old enough, that is, to become besotted by a pair of baby blue eyes. Her name was Johanna and she lived in the house across the way. Of German descent, she was the target of the local bullies, whose taunting frequently brought tears to her eyes. Her plight touched John deeply until he became besotted, spending more and more time with her, and less and less with me.

One autumn afternoon, we were dawdling home together, shuffling our feet through the piles of fallen leaves, when we rounded a corner and there the bullies were, ranged in cruel formation around her. I walked on but John grabbed me by the coat and held me to the spot.

"We've got to rescue her!" he exclaimed.

I Remember Me

"But they're bigger'n us," I protested, "and there's lots of 'em!"

"I'll go by myself, then, if you won't come!"

Visions of his broken and bruised body floated before me and it would be all my fault if I refused to help. After all, he was my brother and if he loved her, then I loved her as well. I couldn't leave him to face his fate alone. "I'm coming too!" I declared.

Like a pair of chivalrous knights, we set out to avenge her, our very own damsel in distress. Soundlessly, we filled our pockets with stones, then crept up behind her persecutors and pelted them for all we were worth. In that brief moment while surprise stunned their senses, we grabbed her and were off, running like foxes from the hounds until finally we went to ground a safe distance away.

They fanned out in formation, thrashing at the bracken and bushes with sticks. Hearts pounding, we stayed stock still for what seemed an eternity, listening until the last of their footsteps thudded away into the distance. Safe at last, we burst into hysterical laughter, exhilarated by our victory, and Johanna rewarded us with cuddles and kisses. Arm in arm, her dashing heroes escorted her home.

Then, to John's utter dismay, Johanna left town. With relief, I returned happily to riding my scooter but John, as if in his misery he were enlisting in the foreign legion, joined the cubs to forget. He rose through the ranks to become a senior-sixer and it was only natural that I, as his henchman, should also enlist as a cub when my time came.

♪♫♪♫♪

I hold no pretence to a liking for school. My happiest hours there came when the air raid sirens screamed their orders to down books and head for the shelters. We had two of these concrete fortifications in our schoolyard, both above ground. We'd stream out of the classroom and file our way in, a hundred noisy kids and their overwrought teachers in each.

To the unmusical accompaniment of battle-mania, we would launch into song. I sang, with much gusto, songs like *Ten Green Bottles*, *One Man Went to Mow*, *Ten in the Bed* and many others that echoed off the shelter walls. These songs were cleverly designed to teach us basic arithmetic, but the devilishly disguised digits didn't fool me for a minute. Eventually, because I had the loudest voice, I found myself leading the singing. The battle-weary teachers seemed more than pleased to leave it to me, and I gained the admiration of my classmates by switching to the more popular

The Morning of my Life

songs of the day, like *My Bonny Lies Over the Ocean*, *The Quartermaster's Store* and *Mares Eat Oats*.

I revelled in this, my debut performance to a live audience. It gave me a sensation of power to be able to hold the attention of so many through sheer vocal volume and verve.

One day, emerging from the shelter following the all clear, I was just in the nick of time to witness an enemy airman who had parachuted into our playground. I knew for sure that he was a NAZI and I would have descended upon him but for the ARP wardens who quickly ushered him away. For weeks after, we all bragged about what we would have done to the hapless airman, if given the chance.

Privately, I felt puzzled to find the bewildered German pilot appeared to be just a frightened young man, no different from any of our own. I'd expected to be confronted with some kind of monster. Way in the back of my mind, I recall a blackboard with cartoon-style chalk drawings depicting the Nazis as pigs in uniform and it's evident I'd become a victim of the brainwashing so prevalent in my schooldays.

A rare picture of my father, relaxing with a pipe.

Dad always seemed to be working extremely long hours, often away for days at a time, and we saw very little of him. We were curious to know what he did at work and Mum proudly stated he was a very important man in Lucas Laboratories. Gran, however, let us into the secret that he was involved in some sort of hush-hush work. We found this very exciting, believing him to be a secret agent. Spy he wasn't, but he was indeed involved in top secret work absolutely vital to the war effort.

The Rover Company had been contracted to develop the new jet propulsion engine, the brainchild of a young RAF officer named Frank Whittle. Dad was called in to work on the project, which was operating in great secrecy at Waterloo Mill, Clitheroe, in the North West of England.

Engines and power had fascinated Dad since childhood. As a young man, his pride and joy was his Calthorpe motorbike. With his own modifications and inventions applied to it, it was the best competition 350cc machine in Australia, and on it he'd become road racing and hill climb champion, at one time holding the Australasian record for a quarter mile standing start. It wasn't surprising he found himself in his element, working on the new jet engine.

I am proud to say it was my father who was the inventor of the jet's intricate fuel systems. The prototype, the W2B, flew in 1941 but it took until 1944 before it went into service for the RAF as the Rolls-Royce Derwent engine, powering the first British jet fighter, the Gloster Meteor, the first aeroplane to exceed 600 mph.

Of course, we knew nothing of this at the time. To us, he was just our dad - a gentle, generous man who inspired the trust and wide-eyed admiration of us all. His laugh was wonderfully infectious - more of a giggle than a guffaw - and each of his sons seem to have inherited this trait. I remember being so impressed by the laughter lines gracing his eyes I vowed that when I grew up, I would have them too. I spent many moments gazing into the mirror, pinching my face to ensure my creases would form just like his.

As babies, we didn't stimulate his interest for long. It was only as we grew and developed inquiring minds he began to pay us more attention. He always encouraged us to speak out about anything and just about everything, and loved to encourage our curiosity and ingenuity in discovering and learning for ourselves - like the time he instructed us on how to make a crystal-radio set.

I remember watching wide-eyed, while a box of components was emptied on the table in front of us: snaking wires he called cat's whiskers, shiny metal connectors, tuning coils and coloured condensers, a little silvery-grey crystal, looking like a scrap of broken pewter, and many other bits and pieces. My clumsy fingers struggled with the unaccustomed feel

The Morning of my Life

of the screwdriver and I bit my lip in concentration, trying to control the fiddling little components. Finally it was complete and Mum was called to witness the very first twiddle of the cat's whisker upon the crystal. I shall never forget that moment. The indistinct scratching we heard produced was true magic at work, because it was something created by our own hands.

Occasions such as these spent with Dad are, each one, preserved in a special corner of my memory, more precious since they were so few and far between. His work was all-important and almost totally occupied his interest and time. This doesn't mean we were ever far from his thoughts - and we were certainly never bored or lonely.

Our house was always full. I cannot remember anything other than being surrounded by the warmth and activity of a large family. At this time, there was Mum and Dad, we three older boys, plus our baby brother Robert - but it didn't end there. The family spanned two more generations, because living with us was my Gran (Mum's mother, Bessie) and Gran's father, John McGregor. What a lucky lad I was. How many kids can claim the privilege of growing up with not only their gran, but also their very own great-grandfather?

Gran and her father had come over from Australia to visit us before the war, but the outbreak of hostilities had prevented them returning home, so here they were, destined to be with us for the duration. Not only had they come to see Mum and her growing family, but also to revisit their roots - for both of them were born in the village of Walton-le-Dale near Preston in Lancashire.

In 1911, at the age of twenty-two, Gran, who was the eldest of six, had married cotton-mill overseer, William Calbraith Livesey. Soon afterwards, John McGregor, being an adventurous man, decided the family should emigrate to Australia. They sold off their 'Ham & Beef' shop in Lancashire and with the proceeds, purchased their passage. Gran and her husband decided to go with them.

Unfortunately, they were to be together in Australia for only a few years before she was widowed. William, having enlisted in the Australian army, fell on the foreign soil of Ypres in Belgium in 1918. Left alone in a strange country with a two-year-old son, Ken, and baby daughter, Muriel, she settled with her father in the country village of Camden, New South Wales, where he established a delicatessen shop.

Like my father, Great Granddad McGregor possessed a keen inventive mind. He had introduced the first cinema to Camden, had been the first to have his shop window lit up by electricity and had

I Remember Me

experimented with the freezing of puff pastry, a revolutionary concept to the country folk of Camden. Furthermore, he had another claim to fame that I latched onto as soon as I found out; for it was my Great Granddad who was reputed to have conceived, designed and hand-stitched the very first oval-shaped Rugby football. Now, there's a proud boast for the schoolyard.

What a dashing figure he cut. Always suave and debonair, he was rarely seen without a smart suit, bow tie and a waistcoat, which sported a gold fob watch and chain. Strutting through the streets, he would swing his rolled-up umbrella in time with his sprightly gait. Then suddenly, and seemingly out of character, he'd stoop to pick up from the pavement some little item that had sparkled, or otherwise attracted his attention. These treasures he would pocket to stow away in a secret drawer in his room.

One day he must have been really pleased with me, for I was summoned to his room, where, with an 'open sesame' flourish of his arms, this magical drawer was revealed to me in all its splendour.

The suave, debonair figure of my great grandfather, John McGregor, pictured here with his wife, my gran's mother, whom I never knew.

"You may have any item your heart desires!"

I stood transfixed - it was like the proverbial Aladdin's Cave. Here were shiny silver sixpenny pieces, multicoloured marbles and a splendid array of boy's delights that would make even the mines of King Solomon fade by comparison. I can't recall the gift I selected, but I've kept every enchanted recollection of him stowed away in the magical treasure box of my memory.

All too soon this grand old gentleman began to wander in mind and body, taking off at all hours of the day or night saying "I'm going home". I have no recollection of his final departure, other than missing him, and

The Morning of my Life

being told by Gran that he was now at rest. I believe God must have shown him the way home, but not without taking a part of me with him.

♪ ♫ ♪ ♫ ♪

On May 8th 1943, our latest brother Geoffrey Colin decided to join the human race. Soon after, Dad was posted to the Midlands again and took us to live in 100 Wake Green Road, Moseley, Birmingham. This imposing property had two outstanding features simply begging to be explored. The first was an impressive monkey-puzzle tree in the front garden that posed a prickly challenge to all its would-be climbers; but take the challenge I did and bore my scratches like battle scars as evidence of my conquest.

Secondly, there were the cold damp cellars and what a gift these were to the wild imaginings of a gang of lively lads. We made believe they were dungeons, or ghastly torture chambers that could become our secret resistance headquarters if, heaven forbid, England were to be occupied by the foe.

In contrast to the confines of London, these new surroundings offered a freedom to wander and, alone, I would frequent one of my favourite haunts, the River Cole. At the first opportunity, I'd kick off my shoes and wade up and down stream, happily dragging a little net, hoping to snag some red-throated sticklebacks to take home in a jar. Unfortunately, the fish didn't always survive - like the ill-fated ones I placed on the porch wall, only to find next morning that an overnight frost had transformed them into little fishy ice cubes.

I must have been about seven when I became filled with a fascination for ants. I used to collect them in large glass containers filled with earth and kept them beneath my bed so as to watch them tunnel out their nest. Silk worms in boxes soon followed suit. While Mum was willing to suffer my collection of mice in the tool shed, she drew a line at ants and worms in my bedroom, so they had to go.

It was about this time my earliest appreciation of music began to emerge. Stimulated by some old Australian phonograph recordings and Gran's wind-up gramophone, I would jig around the room to the horn blasting out the strains of Peter Dawson singing *Tiny Ball On End Of String* or Albert Whelan's *The Whistler And His Dog*.

I also began to take an avid interest in the wireless. Like the rest of Britain, my ears were glued every evening to the adventures of Dick, Jock and Snowy in *Dick Barton - Special Agent*. Yet I was enthralled even more

I Remember Me

by music, especially the music known as 'Western Style', played by Canadian singer Big Bill Campbell and his Rocky Mountaineers. This was indeed 'mighty-fine' music to my untrained ears and I listened intently, learning the songs off by heart. I went around the house singing them, songs like *Old Paint, You Are My Sunshine* and *I Miss My Swiss* - the latter being my first exposure to the art of yodelling.

Soon I got the opportunity to try this out for myself. Needing the money to enlarge our meagre record collection with some of my own, I took a job as a milkman's assistant. Out on the streets, I'd deliver the milk with a resounding "milk-o-lady-o" and I'm not at all sure the customers appreciated being awoken in the early hours by a young lad's attempt to yodel. Certainly, the stupid old draft horse pulling the milk cart didn't, for one morning he brought the full weight of his hoof down upon my foot. Instantly redundant, I found myself yodelling in agony all the way back home. Ever afterwards, I left the citizens of Moseley to slumber on in peace.

♪ ♫ ♪ ♫ ♪

On May 10th 1945, my new baby brother, David, made his arrival and families all over Britain took to the streets by the million, singing and dancing in joy. Was it mere coincidence Hitler chose this time to throw in the towel, and war in Europe was finally declared over?

I was seven and a half years old and peace was a concept I knew nothing about. It was our Colin who voiced our confusion when one night, after a violent thunderstorm, he asked, "Why aren't the buildings falling down?"

Peace brought a return to more innocent pleasures and war was reduced to the annual autumnal battle of the conker. One day, in search of ammunition, we stopped at the gate of a nearby garden and gazed wistfully at the bulging crop on a magnificent horse-chestnut tree. Greed finally overcame caution and in we went through the gate and marched up to the tree. We were so engrossed in attacking the branches with missiles, attempting to knock down as many conkers as we could, that we didn't see the owner come up upon us until too late.

"You'll never get them like that, boys."

We turned, red-faced, to see a bespectacled little grey-haired lady standing arms akimbo, staring at the tree.

"Look, the best way is to shin up the tree so you can pick off the biggest. That's what I did when I was your age."

Her statement struck me as strange, not only because it was so unexpected - grown-ups had always told me off before for getting into mischief - but also because, previously, I hadn't considered that any adult was ever my age.

"Don't just stand there, lads. Haven't you ever climbed a tree before, or do you need me to show you how?"

We didn't need to be told twice. We shinned up the tree, stripping it of its most valuable assets for all we were worth. When we had garnered all we could carry, we shouted our thanks and ran off with our gains.

Mrs Nichols was the lady's name, and we rewarded her by bestowing upon her the highest accolade we could give - honorary membership of our gang. I think, of all of us, I was the one who valued her friendship the most. She was a widow, living on her own, and on my frequent visits she would always invite me in for tea and cucumber sandwiches, where together we would swap the events of our day.

The morning following my ninth birthday, I rushed over to share a piece of birthday cake with her and to show off my presents. I wore my gift from Mum and Dad - a new pair of shorts - with the hanky from Gran in my pocket, and in my hand I carried the present from my brothers, a boxed set of assorted English road traffic signs. In a tête-à-tête over tea and cake, I informed her that I suspected my Mum and Dad were making plans for us all to go to Australia.

Naturally, there had always been a lot of talk of Australia at home, and now I was getting older, I was beginning to take more interest in what was being said. Lately, I had detected pangs of homesickness in both parents and had heard mention of moving, and ships, and a new life for us boys.

My suspicions were confirmed when not long afterwards, Dad officially announced to us that our sea passage had been booked, and the leaving was imminent. Yes, we were definitely going to live in Australia.

It can't have been an easy decision for my father to make. Certainly he wanted to return home, as did Mum, to see his parents again before they died, and to show them his growing family - but at what cost? Apart from the upheaval and expense of the enterprise, he had fathered a family of English boys, and was taking us away from the security of the home he had worked so hard to provide for us – and for what?

In a word, opportunity - the chance for us to escape the ravages of post-war Britain, to grow up enjoying the healthy free-and-easy lifestyle he had known himself and to benefit from the opportunities offered by a young and vibrant nation.

I Remember Me

But most importantly, he needed a new challenge for himself. Dad had certainly forged his mark in England, and Lucas didn't want to lose him. They offered many inducements to make him change his mind and stay, yet he was adamant about leaving. Finally a compromise had been reached. They concluded a deal whereby he would continue to work for Lucas by setting up and heading a new research and development laboratory for them in Sydney, Australia.

So it was explained to us we were all going to the Antipodes; it was a long way away, but Australia was our home; it was where we all belonged.

There followed a frenzy of preparation and packing, but the enormity of the undertaking was just too great for me to understand, and so I happily let it wash over me until the morning of the sale. The house and all the furniture and possessions we could not take with us were to be sold by auction and there they all were, the fabric of my life piled in a jumble for strangers to pick over and take away. Suddenly, it was brought home to me just what the leaving meant. I wandered among the items, touching and prodding until, half-buried by a pile of boxed games, I came across my most treasured possession - the wooden stool my father had made for me. The entire vista of my nine years became encapsulated in that one little stool. I burst into tears, desperate it shouldn't go to a stranger; it would be like selling my life away. Who then could be entrusted with it?

Mrs Nichols! As soon as I saw her familiar figure on the path, I rushed at her, and dragged her over to where she could best see my precious stool. I said nothing, but I willed her to rescue it for me. She smiled that secret smile at me, squeezed my hand and then left me while she wandered off to view our goods.

I lost sight of her until a while later when I saw her departing. Under her arm she carried her purchase - it was my little stool. Although I was mortified to see it go, I was nevertheless delighted it was going to a good home with my dear friend. She couldn't have had any real use for it, so I believed in my heart - and still do - that she wanted it as a keepsake in memory of the good times we had shared.

Many years later, all grown up and returned to England, I revisited Moseley with high hopes of seeing her once more. I found her still living in the same house. Time hadn't changed her much - she still had that familiar kind face even though now it was framed by silver hair. And do you know what? - to my astonishment she still had my little wooden stool. I recognised it at once, standing majestically like a throne in the corner of her conservatory and still bearing the initials 'FI' I'd etched into its seat. As I gazed at it, my childhood came flooding back to me. My eyes met

The Morning of my Life

hers and we were instantaneously flashed back across the years. I knew then that, to her, I would always be the little lad who had once come scrumping from her conker tree.

♪♫♪♫♪

Time soon dictated our leaving, and the days after Christmas were spent in a round of sad partings. So many people wished to see us off that Dad chartered a bus from Birmingham to Tilbury docks so our friends could travel with us and we, along with our luggage, would arrive in good time for our voyage. We set off before daybreak on a snowy morning and stopped off en-route to collect various friends' bon-voyage kisses and well wishes for the adventure that lay ahead.

A fine group of English boys. My brothers and I in the garden of our home in Moseley, shortly before we left for Australia.
Back row (left to right): John, Jim and me.
Middle: Colin (left) Robert (right). Front: David

- 2 -

LET'S TAKE THE LONG WAY AROUND THE WORLD

The closer I got, the bigger it grew. The immense bulk of the SS Orion loomed before me, towering so high I had to crane my neck just to look up the side of its hull. As for the superstructure, it was so far above, it disappeared from view.

On the other hand, once I was over the gangplank, the proportions were reversed and I felt like a ferret burrowing through a warren of passageways, bulkheads and doors. Once we had found our allotted cabin, we peeked in, threw our hand baggage onto the bunks and made a dash for the top deck.

There, high above the quay, I was pinned against the rails, trying to pick out familiar faces on the dockside below. Reeling with excitement, I turned to share it with Dad, Mum and Gran. Mum smiled back at me, but behind her smile there were tears. Puzzled, I turned to look at Gran, also wet-eyed, then at Dad, surprised even he was obviously battling with an emotion I couldn't understand. Why were they all so sad?

Suddenly, a strident blast shook the ship and we, and all the people on the dock, jumped simultaneously. The monstrous vessel was stirring from its sleep and had begun to come alive, with steam belching from its mighty funnels. Taking their cue, the cheering crowd started to throw ribbons of flimsy streamers, holding them tightly in a futile attempt to impede the progress of the ponderous giant. I waved madly while faces slowly faded into the blurring mass of the disappearing dockyard. It was only then I understood why the grown-ups were feeling sad, for as I watched the banks of the Thames slip away, it dawned on me I was leaving all the friends I had ever known, and might never see again.

Overwhelmed, I tightened my grip onto what could only be described as my security blanket - the only memento of the life I was leaving behind - a box of toy traffic signs. Before leaving, Dad had ruled that we could each take only one item on the voyage, stressing that any more may well scuttle the ship. This difficult choice had placed me in quite a quandary. My toy monkey and I had been inseparable nearly all of my life, but, by now, it was all too obvious that he was suffering from too much cuddling - half the stuffing had gone, one eye was missing altogether, and his tail hung precariously by a single thread. I felt a traitor as I turned my attention to the toy farmyard, but I rejected that too, since the little animals were useless without the model railway set. So, after much painful deliberation, I settled for my birthday present traffic signs, and printed my name boldly on the box.

My moment of melancholy was soon forgotten when my brothers grabbed me, and we raced off to explore. A sextet of pirates bold, we swarmed all over the ship, running amok and repelling all boarders. After a few hours of rioting, we buccaneers had the vessel well sussed out and I resolved to take myself off on my own for a quiet game of make-believe. I found an empty matchbox to use as a car, and went to fetch the little signs, but... they'd gone! My screams soared into supersonic mode and, as they reached their climatic crescendo, I let loose the primeval cry, "MUM!"

Just then, through my panic, I heard the echo of my own name - MY name - being announced over the loud speaker.

"Would Master Ifield please come to the information desk to collect his traffic signs?"

'Master Ifield' eh? I mustered all the composure that this profound moment demanded and strode towards the purser's office, head held proud, swaggering under the grand title of 'MASTER IFIELD'.

♪ ♫ ♪ ♫ ♪

My brothers and I proved to be able seafarers, quite unaffected by the constant rolling of the watery world around us, and soon settled down to the peaceful pace of life on board. Watching and absorbing what was happening around me, I was learning far more than I would have from any stodgy old school. The atlas became reality as we skirted France, Spain and Portugal, and passed through the Straits of Gibraltar into the Mediterranean.

The temperature rose radically. We cruised the coast of North Africa and proceeded via Port Said into the Suez Canal and here, half-blinded by the sun's reflection, I saw the Egyptian and Arabian deserts. Not only saw them, but also experienced the fierceness of their climate - a cruel searing heat, hell-bent on extracting every last vestige of moisture from my puny little English body.

One day, staring at the shore, we gulped at the sight of some policemen who were shooting at a man staggering along in a frantic attempt to flee for his life. Horror-stricken, we saw him fall, maybe killed. I was mortified; this was so contrary to the values I'd been brought up to believe in, and I wondered just what this journey was leading me to.

I Remember Me

But the mighty *Orion* gave no heed as it plodded on, into the Red Sea. Now the view became monotonous - a vast expanse of desert over to the port side and even more sandy waste to starboard. It was a great relief to reach Aden. Here, traders came on board with their model elephants and coiled cobra ash trays carved from solid ebony and ivory. Their ancient skills were exquisite and Mum and Dad purchased some as keepsakes which today still remind us of this great expedition. Then with Aden behind us, the great ship steamed out into the Indian Ocean towards Ceylon, where we were told we would be able to go ashore. Excitement mounted as we docked in the capital Colombo and I could hardly wait to escape from the confines of the ship.

As soon as we disembarked, I was overcome by an unhealthy stench. Millions of flies seemed to rule as kings over the poor wretched people, who existed in squalor in their midst. Miserable beggars plagued us, with deformed babes in their arms, craving money or food scraps. They stared at me, laughing and touching my hair with their filthy fingers. I assume they were just intrigued by my fairness, but I was frightened and tried to avoid them, squirming out of reach of their outstretched hands. I was glad when our brief shore adventure ended and we could get underway once more.

Life on board was never boring as there was so much to do to - deck quoits, table tennis, games, film shows, 'housie-housie' and the music shows I found myself drawn to, as I loved to join in with the sing-alongs.

One day, Gran had us all scrubbed clean and dressed in our best for a right-royal occasion: King Neptune was to present us with diplomas for crossing the Equator. I stood in line with my brothers before this olive green denizen of the deep whose wild eyes glared at us from a tangle of hair and beard, all matted with seaweed. I admit to being apprehensive at the thought of confronting him, but knew I had to put on a brave front for the sake of my younger brothers. When it was my turn, he beckoned me with his trident, and as I stepped forward, his crown slid down at a crooked angle over his greasy forehead and I was enveloped in whisky-soaked fumes. I stared at him in disgust. He held out the scroll, I grabbed it, mumbled my thanks and scurried away.

"He's a bit scary," I admitted to Gran afterwards.

"Pay him no never-mind," she said, "I'm here, and he daresn't mess with me, else I shall swing on his whiskers." Gran was forever threatening to swing on people's whiskers, even if they were clean-shaven, but at least it banished my fears.

Lets Take The Long Way Round The World

After crossing the Equator, we headed south, our massive ship a mere microscopic dot in the mighty expanse of water that stretched to infinity on every side. From time to time, an escort of porpoise and dolphin would accompany us and I'd rush to the rails to watch them frolicking in the ship's wake. Then there were the acrobatic antics of the shoals of flying fish skipping over the surface of the water to escape the ship, as if it were some gigantic predator.

Back in England, whenever we went on long car journeys to the seaside, we played a game that the first to see the sea would win a penny. Now the game was reversed as, from this point on, we kept our eyes glued on the southern horizon for a sign of land. Any formation or shadow in the distance brought the cry "Land Ho!" - but no, it was just another false alarm.

What a let down it was, when it was Dad who first sighted land. It wasn't fair, I protested, since he knew exactly where to look - having been there before. Then we all became quiet and watched enthralled, as the distant speck of land grew bigger by the minute.

"Look, boys, now you can see the bush," Dad proudly proclaimed.

I had heard both Mum and Dad on several occasions reminiscing over the beauty of the 'bush'. Now, at last, I was to see it for myself. I gazed into the distance at the shore now filling the entire horizon.

"Where is it Dad?"

"You can't miss it son, it's straight ahead of you."

I was puzzled, for I had been expecting to find *one* bush, albeit maybe a huge and glorious one, but all I could see was an empty coast bordered by rafts of blue-green trees. It slowly dawned on me, this *was* the bush - miles and miles of it. How could I have been so stupid? Gripping tightly to the rail, I plonked my chin on my hands, and stared out to sea, trying to hide the reddening glow of my humiliation.

We seemed a long time approaching. Why, even the gulls had slowed down to a hover in order to keep pace. They acted just like a cavalcade, carefully escorting us in, as we eventually docked in the port of Fremantle, near Perth, Western Australia.

Unfortunately, disaster befell me and I wasn't able to greet the momentous occasion of our first landfall in the Promised Land with the enthusiasm it deserved. I'd been pigging out on mangoes, papaya, passion fruit, grapes, persimmons, bananas and many other unbelievable fruits of every conceivable colour and shape. I'd never seen such a strange and exotic abundance before and my appetite had been insatiable. But now I

I Remember Me

was paying the price for my greed, swamped by waves of giddiness and battling the pains that clawed at my stomach.

After the ship docked, Dad went ashore to clear customs and immigration. Unaware of my sickly state, he'd left strict instructions for me to wait on deck for his return. He seemed to be gone forever. Left alone with my grumbling tummy, I felt afraid and abandoned, and began to panic. Ignoring his instructions, I ran off down the ramp and onto the quay.

I careered blindly amid the lofty, sun-tanned Aussies, with their "g-day"s and "ow-y-goin-mate"s, and cannoned slap-bang into a docker's stomach. He grabbed me in a pair of muscle-bound arms and raised me aloft as easily as lifting a cotton wool ball.

"Stone the crows bluey - wot's ya 'urry?"

Then he grinned, for he had sussed that all was not well with my internal workings. He sat me astride a pile of sacked potatoes and offered a magic powder in a mug of water. Obediently I drank, and - bingo! - instantaneous wellness. He chuckled at my deep sigh of relief, tousled my hair with his sandpaper fingers and introduced himself as Bazza. After I had thanked him for his kindness, we chatted meaningfully together, man to man, while we awaited Dad's return.

"There he is now," I shouted, pointing as Dad emerged from the crowd. I leapt from the pile of potatoes and ran to him.

Mr Bazza followed closely behind. "Don't do ya block with the nipper mate, 'es bin pretty crook - almost chundered, but everything's jake now - ain't it sport?"

Without waiting for an answer, he turned and threw a wink at me over his shoulder saying, "See-ya's later - hooroo."

Then he was gone.

I hadn't understood a word of what Mr Bazza had said, but I assumed Dad must have, because I heard no more about it - much to my relief.

Thanks to Mr Bazza, I was assured Australia was a comfortable and welcoming place, and any worries I'd been harbouring after our experiences on the way, were banished. I trotted off along the quay, perfectly recovered and alert to all the sights and sounds of my new surroundings.

We went out of the docks into the town, Dad sauntering along with his hands clasped behind his back and the rest of us following in a troupe behind him. I wondered why all the shops had awnings out, even though the sapphire sky promised not a drop of rain. I understood the reason as soon as I stepped into their shade, grateful to be out of the heat of the sun. The shops were heaped with goods, quite unlike English stores - and all available without a ration card, Dad explained. I was only half listening, for I was staring at the men casually strolling around, beer in hand. Most of them wore shorts, something rarely seen in England, and some were without shirts; most wore thongs on their feet, while some even went barefooted. I squinted out into the wide sun-drenched streets, where the glare off the white buildings dazzled me. The air tasted clean and sweet, after weeks of salt sea breezes, and I could smell exotic scents brought on the wind from the masses of many-hued flowers that seemed to be everywhere.

All too soon, we had to return to the ship and I was surprised to find, although we had finally reached Australia, our destination was still many days away. We called in briefly at Adelaide and Melbourne, and then slowly, painfully slowly, sailed the shores of eastern Victoria and headed north, up the coast of New South Wales. At last, we skirted the long jutting peninsular of South Head, turned west through the harbour entrance and into a glittering waterway fringed by a welter of craggy inlets. The sky arched deep blue over a flotilla of yachts, so bright they seemed like little white dots embossed on the surface of the sea.

Sydney Harbour Bridge

Then finally, we rounded a headland - and WOW! It seemed we were passing through the portals of heaven itself, as there before me stood the shining city of Sydney, proudly wearing its majestic metallic crown - the Great Harbour Bridge.

I Remember Me

So this was Sydney. I stood motionless, entranced, until I felt my father's hand on my shoulder and heard him proudly proclaim, "There you are boys, we've arrived home".

Home? I really couldn't grasp it. Until this moment, the word 'home' had been synonymous with the familiar streets of London and Birmingham. Now here I was, face to face with another world Down Under, a land whose existence I had only ever dreamed of, and was being told that this was 'home'.

Was I really home? Well, yes indeed. Since home is where the heart is, and my heart was with my family, I was home. After all, I am of genuine Australian stock. Yet I was born in England and the land that gave me birth will forever evoke childhood memories that kindle warm feelings within me.

- 3 -
WHERE I AM COMING FROM

I stared in total disbelief. Gosh! It was hardly a proper car - it looked like a reject from an American gangster movie. Beneath all the rust and mud, its box-shaped hulk was a sort of dark blue and on its nickel-plated radiator grill, it sported a hexagonal badge proclaiming it to be an "Essex Super Six".

Uncle Frank, a tall, wiry, thin-faced man with a smile as broad as the brim of his hat, opened the front passenger door and politely guided Mum's step onto the huge running board. Uncle Frank was the husband of Dad's sister Vera and had come to Pyrmont docks in order to convey us to our first destination, a place with the very English-sounding name of 'Exeter'. It was a distance of some hundred miles, and I wondered how his amazing rattletrap would get us there.

Gran had been met by her sister Mary and husband Lance and had gone off to stay with them for a while. It still left a crowd of us to accommodate in the car. Astonishingly, there was easily room for us all. Mum and Dad clambered onto the front bench seat, while we six kids piled into the back, which was so high we could even stand up. Above my head gaped a large hole in the canvas roof, and I spied an umbrella I guessed had been placed at hand in case it rained. Uncle Frank turned the key, breathing life into the engine's six cylinders, and after a belch of black smoke, we were under way.

We drove at an amazing pace, tyres squealing as we swerved in and out of the tram-tracks like a dodgem at the fair. The streets of Sydney seemed unexpectedly narrow, and wound higgledy-piggledy around rivers and inlets. Everywhere were flowers, huge tropical blossoms whose scent filled the air. In the city, we passed terraced town houses decorated with filigree wrought-iron work while, in the suburbs, bungalows with wide, shady verandas spread out around us, and tumbledown dwellings with rusty corrugated iron roofs, looking as though the inhabitants weren't sure they would stay.

Eventually, we emerged into open countryside. I screwed up my eyes and peered out of the open sides of the car, but there were only grazing sheep and a few dead gum trees to be seen.

I'd begun to doze in the heat and sway of the car, when suddenly an excited cry from Mum roused me as we rattled into the town of Camden.

"This is where your great-grandfather once lived."

I Remember Me

I sat up and took note as Mum pointed out places such as the delicatessen shop and the Empire Theatre, formerly named Forrester's Hall, where he had introduced moving pictures or 'flickers' as they were known then.

With Camden behind us, we started to ascend the foothills of the Great Divide, with the bushland becoming more dense and the air sweet and cool as we wound around the Razorback hills of Picton. At last, I spotted a sign reading 'Moss Vale' and 'Bowral' with, seemingly like an afterthought in smaller print, our destination, 'Exeter'.

Uncle Frank brought the jalopy to a halt and we tumbled out. Stiff and subdued after the journey, we stood blinking with uncertainty at the quaint little house with its shaded front porch, snoozing in the sun. Then, with a whoop and a holler, I raced across the yard, setting off a tirade of squawking from the startled chooks that scurried away, feathers flying. The fly screen door was flung wide with a clang and out stepped a rather reserved lady, who stood stiffly to attention with a fixed smile, as if she were about to have her photo taken. Close behind followed a fine old gentleman, tall and lean with his trousers belted up by a piece of frayed rope. He sauntered slowly forward, with a welcoming grin, and I realised we were in the presence of our very own Grandma and Grandpa Ifield.

Hugs and greetings over, they ushered us inside their little house. Bags, boxes and cases were unpacked and before long we had crammed our belongings into every nook and cranny of their tidy home, pushing its protesting walls to the limit. Indeed, we even overflowed into a tent that had to be hastily erected to cope with our invasion.

Early next morning, while Grandpa relaxed in his rocking chair on the porch, we went through our party tricks on the lawn. Jim ran and jumped about, while John turned cartwheels.

"Can you do this Grandpa?" they skited.

"Yep" came the reply.

Not to be outdone, I followed, demonstrating my skills with steady head stands, while the contents of my pockets dropped out like hail stones all around me. "How about this Grandpa, can you do this too?"

"Yep" was the brief response, from an equally upside down Grandpa.

We were impressed that such an aged gentleman could have such energy - and in fact it was precisely because of his eternal 'pep' that he'd acquired the nickname Peppa. He was indeed a colourful character - a man's-man, forged from tough pioneering stock, yet he had a soft, gentle manner and an ever-ready smile, deepened by the weather-beaten lines of his rough-shaven face. To me, he was the personification of the great Australian trailblazer.

Like he was the Pied Piper, we kids followed him everywhere, as he took it upon himself to teach us the wonders of the Great Australian Bush, and to equip us with its skills. Down at the swimming hole we went skinny-dipping, and he showed us how to catch yabbies from the creek. These freshwater crayfish were lured by dangling a small chunk of raw meat on the end of a string, until the poor creature could contain itself no longer and its claw reached to grab the bait - and there it was, another for the pot.

He also taught us how to carve the Australian mulga wood. I tried to fashion several works of art, chipping away at the timber, sanding and buffing it with boot polish to enhance its yellow and brown grain, but they always seemed to end up as rough ashtrays or book ends.

With Peppa as tutor, I became inspired to be either a carpenter or a bushman. Reading, writing, arithmetic and other such mundane subjects were far from my thoughts, until one evening at supper, Dad uttered that dreaded word, "school".

"Oh Dad..." I whinged, and stopped mid-sentence to heave a sigh of disgust. A grim vision of College Road School in England came drifting back across the ether, with the matriarchal presence of Miss Mason and draughty classrooms redolent with the smell of chalk dust and boiled cabbage.

However, the image faded on first sight of the friendly little bush school, nestling under the gum trees. This rustic building, fashioned from roughly sawn timber, had a shady veranda at one end, where the sinks and drinking bubblers were fed from a rainwater tank. The communal toilet was about a hundred yards further down the field. This smelly little blow-fly haven, called a dunny, discouraged anyone from lingering. I could imagine in wintertime it might seem a hundred yards too far away, but here, in high summer, it was a hundred yards too close.

We walked to school, but most of the other dozen or so pupils arrived on horseback. Their ponies were tethered to the slip-rails, and later let loose to feed in the adjoining paddock, reminding me of the western movies. I can't remember the lessons in the classroom, but from the other kids we learnt plenty. They showed us how to differentiate between the poisonous trapdoor-spiders' holes and those of the harmless cicadas. We'd pour water down these holes to force the insect to the surface and watch the miracle as it emerged from the dark into a myriad of pristine colours. They taught us to recognise them all, from the miniature black Peter-Peter

I Remember Me

to the colourful Green Grocer, Black Prince, Floury Baker, Cherry Nose, Yellow Monday and the Double Drummer that managed to make twice as much noise as all the others combined.

Meanwhile, my education at Peppa's hands continued apace. Every evening he'd sit on the veranda, his rocker swaying in time to the rhythmic chirping of the crickets. While he whittled away at a piece of wood and slurped contentedly on his pipe, I'd squat by his side, chewing on a paspalum straw.

One evening he drew my attention to the ring on his finger saying, "There, Frank, look at that." As I gazed into the fiery black opal, he said, "I gouged for that myself. Yes, and hard times they were too my lad." Mesmerised, I watched the iridescent flame dancing within the huge gemstone, while he settled back to tell me of the great depression years when he had spent time as a gouger in search of opals at Lightning Ridge, near the Queensland border.

Another evening, a strange light came into his eyes. In his mind, he was back in Tumbaroora, which lay downstream from its sister gold town of Hill End, somewhere between Hargraves and Bathurst, out west beyond the Blue Mountains. It's a no-account place today, but in its heyday it was a boomtown, boasting a dozen hotels. Peppa had been there, joining the desperate in their search for that elusive fortune. "Why, I've even seen men lift coffins from the graves, to rummage for gold beneath them," he told me.

He went on to explain how two German prospectors had taught him to pan at their claim in the bend of the river. Suddenly, he turned and grabbed my arm, a look of fanaticism on his face. "I was there when they discovered the largest solid gold nugget I have ever seen," he declared. "Those Germans gifted me their claim site and moved on further downstream, but I was convinced there was still more gold there - and there was!"

Then his eyes widened and his voice dropped to a whisper as he confided, "I reckon I discovered an actual reef of gold. One of these days, I'll take you there and show you."

It was obvious to me he was still suffering from gold fever.

On another evening, he talked of the horse-drawn coaches of Cobb & Co that, even at the turn of the century, were the main means of travelling to the country areas.

"Did you ride in them, Grandpa?" I wanted to know.

"Ride in them! Why, I crossed the country in them, many times over."

Where I Am Coming From

It transpired that Peppa, in addition to being an opal gouger and gold prospector, had also been a member of a travelling minstrel show, touring the isolated townships, where they'd put on a show for the country folk.

He puffed out his chest and announced, "I was Mr Interlocutor, Master of Ceremonies."

Not sure what that involved, I asked, "What did you do?"

Suddenly he got to his feet, pushed back his chair and tap-danced along the verandah, the boards, bouncing and squeaking under his tapping feet. Everyone came out to see what the noise was and watched, astounded by the old man's agility. Then, with little sign of breathlessness despite the ravages of time, he burst into song.

I was astonished, impressed and inspired. Never mind the bushman or the carpenter, this was what I wanted to be - a singer like my granddad.

Now, every evening I would pester him to sing some more while I joined in the choruses. Patiently, he taught me some of his songs, such as *The Chivalrous Man-eating Shark*, *Rock All The Babies To Sleep*, *The Little Shirt My Mother Made for Me*, *The Cat Came Back* and a beautiful ballad called *Molly Darling*.

"I learnt that one, son, when I was a sailor in the Irish merchant navy."

"Irish?" I asked, in surprise.

"Yeah, that's right. Mind you, in order to get the job, I had to pretend I was an Irishman," and he demonstrated for me, in a truly believable brogue. "I had to keep up the charade the whole time - for if they'd found me out, I would have been skinned alive."

Grandpa was full of wondrous tales, not just of his own exploits, but also of the pioneering history of Australia. I lay on my front, with my chin propped up on my hands, all ears, while I took in the exciting stories of pioneer gold diggers, bandits and outlaws, highway robbery and gun battles on horseback. It was just like the movies, only this was real, because it happened here - and my own ancestors were part of it. Peppa's proud boast was that his mother, Elizabeth Nelson, was the daughter of the Australian hero, Constable Samuel Nelson.

The story goes that in 1865 Nelson, my great-great-grandfather, was stationed at the little town of Collector, near Goulburn, New South Wales. It was the time of the great Australian Gold Rush, when gangs of bandits, or 'bushrangers' as they were called, roamed the bush. They held themselves beyond the law, eluding capture at the hands of the troopers and the police, despite the high price on their heads. One of the most celebrated of the outlaws was the notorious Ben Hall.

I Remember Me

Ben and his gang of cut-throats - Dunn, Gilbert, Burke and Vane – rode into town one day when Constable Nelson was on duty all alone. They entered the Kimberley Inn, where Hall menaced the proprietor with his pistol demanding a meal, and the rest of the them rounded up the few customers and locked them in a room at the rear of the hotel. Despite being outnumbered five to one, Constable Nelson did not hesitate. He grabbed his carbine and hurried purposefully towards the hotel. Without giving him a chance to defend himself, gang member John Dunn shot him straight through the heart and left him to die on the street. This cold-blooded killing enraged the whole country and led eventually to the arrest and execution of John Dunn, and the capture and death of Ben Hall himself.

Grandpa concluded his tale by saying: "Why, even today, the people of Collector are very proud of the brave and fearless Constable Nelson, and have erected a monument in his memory."

The people of Collector erected a monument to my great-great-grandfather, Samuel Nelson. The monument as it is today.

Where I Am Coming From

Many years later I went to Collector, a small town near Goulburn, to see for myself the granite monument erected in 1907 in commemoration of my great-great-grandfather's brave deed.

Grandpa also told me that if I cared to look on the map, I would see a district of north Goulburn, marked as 'Ifield'. It's the only remaining evidence of a grant of land once bestowed on an ancestor who had immigrated from England. Curious to know just who this noble ancestor was who had planted our name for posterity on the plains of New South Wales, I badgered Grandpa to tell me his story too. But apart from the information that there are two English villages also named Ifield, one in Kent and another in Sussex, I learnt no more. His secrecy only increased the mystery and intrigue.

So fascinated was I that in later years, when I returned to Britain, I set off in search of my heritage. Today the town of Ifield in Sussex lies near the vast international airport at Gatwick. However, it's to the village of Ifield in Kent that I have traced my apparent forebears. This village is now known as 'Ifield and Singlewell', although it appears the name Ifield predates its shared name. The link is a John Ifield, born a Protestant in the year 1801. He was a collar and harness maker, charged with pig stealing and brought to trial at the Kent Quarter Sessions on January 1st 1833 where, in consideration of former convictions, he was sentenced to be transported 'beyond the seas' for seven years. John spent nearly six years of his term in Woolwich Gaol before he was transported to Australia on the convict ship *Bengal Merchant*, arriving in Sydney on July 21st 1838.

So it was from Peppa I learnt of my ancestral background but, more importantly, it was from him that I received my richest inheritance - his love of singing. I was later to perform and record many of those songs I learnt from him, and from his tales of early Australia I was inspired to write *Whiplash*, a song I recorded in 1958 as the theme for the Australian TV series of the same name, featuring stories of Cobb & Co during those early pioneering days.

In 1851, the great Australian Gold rush
The only law, a gun, the only shelter wild brush
Whiplash - Whiplash - Whiplash
Through mulga wood and desert, the stage thunders by.
From Sydney to Camden and on to Gundagai...

[Whiplash]

Time spent in Exeter with Grandpa and Grandma was all too short. Dad had found us a new home and it was time to hit the road once more. This time, though, our conveyance was not a weird and wondrous

I Remember Me

gangster motor, it was Dad's pride and joy - a 1936 Riley Kestrel, a keepsake of the days when he worked at Riley's.

Of all the possessions we were forced to leave behind, this was one from which he could not bear to be parted, so he'd had it shipped to Australia with us. The regal, gleaming black automobile was a symbol of our old life in England and the comforting smell of her leather upholstery was like an anchor to the past in the midst of a sea of the strange and new. We drove off with dignity, heading up the Old Northern Road, towards Wiseman's Ferry – destination Dural.

- 4 -

BAREFOOT DAYS

"There we are," said Dad, pointing to a large circular water tower, "this is our new home."

After the bizarre experiences we'd been through, I was gullible enough to believe him but it was only after we'd driven past I realised he was kidding. How he laughed – why, even today, I can still hear that giggle of his every time I pass that tower.

We'd already driven through Dural, a small village boasting a school, general store, an ancient Anglican Church and a rustic village hall. Now we were heading through Sydney's orchard belt where not only were there acres of citrus groves sweeping to the left and right of us, but also peaches and nectarines growing in abundance.

Soon we came to a turning on the right where a neglected dirt track joined the main road. Listing drunkenly on its post was a dilapidated sign splattered with shotgun pellets, that read 'Carters Road'. The sign seemed to beckon us, so we obeyed, but it had given no warning of what to expect. Our low slung car, more fitted to the smooth roads of Britain, bashed and battered its way over the ruts, flinging us around inside with a violence that made my teeth judder. However, Dad, the one-time champion dirt track rider, managed to steer around the worst of the potholes, dodging the kamikaze rabbits as he went. The going went from bad to worse until the road all but petered out. Here, in the driveway of a traditional little bushland homestead, we came to a stop.

The homestead was a quaint fibro built bungalow, shaded by wattles, blue gums and a large mulberry tree. It was, however, totally dwarfed by a monstrosity of a gigantic corrugated iron shed which was to become Dad's workshop and office quarters. Here he would continue to work for his English Company and if anyone braved this dead-end road they would be confronted with our new and impressive sign which read 'Lucas Laboratories Propriety Limited'.

It's true, Dad's ramshackle factory was far from being the prettiest building in Australia but to me it was the best for, being that the little bungalow was far too small to accommodate us all, it was under its eaves my brothers and I established our own billets.

I Remember Me

Echidna

Wombat

Goanna

Kookaburra

Some of my companions in the bush at our home in Dural

Barefoot Days

Our new home encompassed not only the bungalow and factory, but also eighty-nine acres of natural bushland. I believe Dad bought this recently released Crown land for as little a ten shillings an acre and it was the best investment he ever made.

I discarded my shoes and took off into the bush at every opportunity. My toes were always anxious to make contact with nature's warm earth and I loved all the different sensations; the feeling of the cool grass, the powdery sand, the sticky mud, the rippling water and even the unyielding crusty rocks. If I had regarded myself as a nature boy back in England, then here I was downright primeval. Stripped to the bare essentials, I would explore my domain, sticking my nose up high to breathe its clean air laden with the heady fragrances of boronia, native roses, flannel flowers and the stunning scarlet waratah, which is the floral emblem of New South Wales.

I was never alone. The flowers attracted an amazing array of exotic birds, ranging from the tiniest humming birds no bigger than a large butterfly, to the huge currawongs and kookaburras. Often, while I clambered through the bush at nesting time, a bird would be cheeky enough to land on me to extract a strand or two of hair or pull lint from my clothing.

One day, while secreted behind some bushes, I was fortunate enough to catch the rare sight of a lyrebird with its tail fanned out and vibrating like the old instrument of its name. Though they are extremely shy, they are great mimics. I have heard them copy not only every other bird call, but the sounds of a crosscut saw, the squeals of children at play and the chopping of wood. Our neighbour once hurt his back lifting a rock and gave a yell that was repeated in the bush for days afterwards.

I've seen mighty goannas, over twelve-foot long, scurry through the undergrowth and up into the trees and I've watched the speed of the echidna burrowing straight down into the ground and out of sight. There were koalas in our wilderness, too, along with wombats and rock wallabies. None of these creatures ever seemed to be harmful or frightening, except for a few snakes and spiders, but the noises I made by walking through the bush generally sent them slithering away.

I loved the bush at any time of day, but it was dusk that impressed me most, when the vast empty skies would fill with the splendour of the magnificent Australian sunset. It was as if a great master painter was at work. Unable to decide which colour to choose next, he would throw onto the canvas every tint from his palette, until the masterpiece reached its glittering finale. This, then, was followed by a velvety blackness packed with stars sparkling so brightly they seemed close enough for me to pluck out with my hand.

♪♫♪♫♪

I longed to experience a sleep-out in the bush, so when Dad came home one day with some army surplus jungle hammocks, complete with roof and mosquito-netted sides, I couldn't wait to try them out. Like explorers in the jungle, my brothers John and Jim and myself set off with our rations and kit, wending our way through the dense undergrowth until we came upon a little gully down by the creek, where we decided to make camp. In the warm glow of sunset we ate our rations and were in bed before nightfall, ready for a good night's sleep.

As I lay there motionless in the eerie moonlight, shadows began to form into menacing shapes of monsters, luminous mushrooms glowed their weird light from the stumps of old trees and the night became alive with sounds - the grunts and groans of frogs, the moaning of the mournful cuckoo, the screech of the nightjar and the rustling of reptiles. This was another world, quite unlike the friendly warmth of the daytime bush. I lay quietly, fighting to keep fear at bay by finding rational explanations for all the weird nocturnal noises. Even when I sensed a gentle tickling on my skin it wasn't beyond my reasoning. I consoled myself by thinking it was only a leaf, a mosquito or maybe a spider.

"SPIDER!"

I froze. Every hair on my body stood on end. I knew about the deadly spiders to be found in these parts.

In a constricted whisper, I called, "John, are you awake?"

No reply.

"Jim, can you hear me?"

Still no response.

There was nothing for it - I would have to make a quick getaway. I rolled over to unzip the netting. All of a sudden, the world revolved and strong, stringy tentacles were grappling me, trapping me upside down in a hanging cocoon. All efforts to be brave evaporated and I let out a wild scream into the night.

My brothers, now very much awake, showed no sympathy but laughed heartily at my plight. However, they did eventually condescend to free me from the tangled mess of upturned hammock and twisted netting. With torches, they instigated a search for the offending spider,

Barefoot Days

only to discover I had been sleeping with a little feather and an overactive imagination.

These were joyous days of discovery. I felt an integral part of creation in the bush, fully alive and aware of the pulsation of life as my heart beat its rhythm to the cicadas' drumming call. Life in England was gradually becoming a fond yet distant memory. I didn't miss city life at all, for I had everything I needed right here.

There was, of course, the family, which since the arrival of my youngest brother, Philip Alan, on May 8th 1948, now numbered seven boys - the largest all male family in the area. Gran was living with us again and soon my beloved Grandpa and Grandma Ifield moved from Exeter into a little old federation house in the neighbouring village of Arcadia.

As a family, we created our own entertainment, singing together, enjoying games and listening to the radio or playing records. Occasionally, we would be treated to a concert or a Saturday afternoon film show at the Dural Memorial Hall. Dural village served a far-flung rural population, made up mainly of orchards and market gardens with a few scattered piggeries and poultry farms. People would supplement their income by trading their surplus produce with their neighbours. Milk was delivered from the local dairy and poured into a churn kept by the roadside.

The family, now seven boys, at our bushland home in Dural.
Back: John, Jim, me. Front: Colin, Robert, Philip, David.

I Remember Me

In an effort to be more self-sufficient, we erected our own chicken coup. There's nothing to compare with freshly laid, free-range eggs swiped from beneath an indignant hen. The rooster never did take kindly to us thieving his goodies. He would threaten us with flapping wings and a menacing battle cry and tackle us head on. However, he didn't last for long. Once he had attacked Dad, a more docile cockerel soon replaced him.

Not only did we have our own chooks but also a pet duck called Henrietta, who attempted, with great difficulty because of her webbed feet, to roost with the hens on the pole at night. One time, I recall seeing a snake caught on the fence around the coop. He had swallowed an egg he must have found on the ground outside, for it was clearly visible as an undigested bulge. Not satisfied, he'd then slithered part way through the chicken wire to devour yet another egg from inside the coop - and there he hung, not able to move, suspended by two eggs, trapped by his own greed. He met his end with one fell swoop of my machete.

♪ ♫ ♪ ♫ ♪

My two elder brothers had been given places at Hornsby High School, while I went with Colin and Robert to the little local primary school in Dural, a prefabricated wooden building housing about thirty-five children.

With our English upbringing we were, much to our embarrassment, objects of curiosity to the native-born Aussie bush kids. I was called 'Pommie bastard' by the school gang of toughs who ragged me incessantly over my funny accent, which puzzled me because, until then, I wasn't aware I had one. So I learned to say 'g'day' and 'hooroo' and used 'bonza' and the occasional 'bloody' thrown in with other of the local vernacular in an attempt to assimilate, but never could achieve the nasal ocker sound. I didn't put up with the intimidation for long. After a few bleeding noses had been exchanged in defence of my brothers and myself, they conceded they had met their match and we became accepted.

At first, a neighbour collected us from the top of Carters Road and dropped us off with his son Roger, but soon I rebelled against the dusty jolting in the back of his pick-up truck. In the sweet air of early morning, the lure of the bush was just too enticing, so I set off with Robert and Colin to carve a three-mile track across the paddocks between home and school.

We'd pass by the piggery, leap over the stile then stride out quickly through the dry grass hoping not to draw the attention of the neighbour's

Barefoot Days

prize bull. Then we'd duck under the straggling saplings, cross the creek and carefully climb over the barbed wire fence, breaking into a run past the old witch's haunted house. A local farmer had told us this myth to deter us from running across his vegetable patch. We half believed his tale because of the eerie look of the deserted building, but it didn't stop us - we just ran faster.

Three inseparable canine companions accompanied us on these daily treks. There was my own trusty fox terrier Laddie, followed by Robert and Colin's hounds, Prince and Sandy, who were two brothers of true blue, mongrel stock - part kelpie and part blue cattle dog. On reaching school, I would point and Laddie would lead the pack straight back home.

When school was out, they would be there waiting and we'd take the same route home, only in reverse. Freed from the clutches of the classroom, I could feel my energy being replenished by the warmth of the sun and would express my ecstasy in song while Laddie's tail doubled as a metronome, beating in time to my singing. Singing was becoming as important as the air I breathed and I let my voice ring out, competing with the trilling of the birds and the chirping of cicadas.

One Saturday morning I whistled for Laddie, who usually came straight to heel, wagging his tail. Prince and Sandy were already panting and rearing to go. I called even louder and soon all my brothers joined me. We fanned out in different directions to search for him, calling loudly as we went. An hour or so passed and still no sign. Mum tried to comfort me by saying "he'll come home when he's hungry, just you wait and see." But I didn't believe her. Laddie had never deserted me before.

Then I saw John coming up from the valley carrying a black and white bundle. I didn't dare guess or want to think what it was until he brought it to me and gently broke the news that Laddie was dead. I snatched the limp body and shrieked hysterically, accusing him of killing my dog, then bolted off through the bush to my own special flat rock, where I poured out my misery, sobbing into the hushed stillness. Eventually I became aware of a sympathetic arm around my shoulder. It was Robert, come to comfort his big brother. We sat in a huddle there for as long as it took to exhaust our tears then I wrapped the now stiffened bundle in my shirt and carried it homeward. Laddie was ceremoniously buried, his grave marked by a personally crafted headstone with the words 'To My Mate' scratched into the sandstone as an epitaph.

Maybe I could be forgiven for reacting unreasonably in the heat of the moment, but I continued to blame John even after I learned a tick caused Laddie's death. This incident had brought to a head an uneasy

I Remember Me

resentment I had already begun to harbour against John. We two, so near in age, had always been inseparable and now we appeared to be drifting apart. Through no fault of his, John was going to a separate school, making new friends and spending less time with me. He was maturing fast and I felt he was growing up and leaving me behind.

I think maybe he sensed this, for he began to join me, along with Prince and Sandy, in our rabbit hunting expeditions where we spent many an hour together roaming the fields, sending the dogs to flush the creatures from their hiding places. Out there, it was song that proved to be the healer, the catalyst for a closer relationship, as we sang together, giving vent to our feelings with no fear of embarrassment.

We made an unbeatable team when it came to rabbiting. The area was alive with them, countless thousands of furry bodies scampering along the paths and foraging busily for nourishment in the grasses of the bush. There was no room here for the sentimental attachment to the pet bunnies our Jim had kept back in England. No, here they were in plague proportions and regarded as vermin - and a legitimate source of income for an enterprising schoolboy, short of cash.

The ones caught on the way to school were left hanging over the fence until our return and, believe me, they couldn't be used for human consumption. However the pelts were fine and would join the rest to be dried over a wire frame and then sold to a visiting dealer. The price for high quality winter pelts once reached as high as one pound per pound weight. It was becoming quite a lucrative business and some local families, who enjoyed rabbit stew, offered a few more shillings to swell my coffers.

The income was much needed as I was desperately trying to amass sufficient pocket money to buy a guitar. The urge to sing was growing so strong that it was not enough on its own; I now had the compelling desire to accompany myself. Indeed, I felt increasingly an insistent urge for music to play a major role in my future - though how, when or where, I had no idea.

-5-

IT ALL BEGAN IN A COWSHED

Rabbit hunting had to be suspended when Dad enlisted our help to remove the undergrowth and scattered rocks from the so-called cleared land at the top of our property. He wouldn't tell us why we were doing it and curiosity prompted excited speculation - maybe we're going to build a new house or, perhaps we're making a paddock and getting a horse for Christmas? Yet despite constant pestering, he didn't let on.

We worked hard over many weekends. Then one morning, to our intense surprise, we saw Dad coming up the drive, leading the lolloping form of a beautiful Jersey cow. She turned her large, moist nose towards me, raised her long, curling eyelashes, and looked me up and down with the biggest and brightest deep brown eyes I had ever seen.

I threw my arm around her neck and asked excitedly, "Are we going to keep her Dad?"

"Yes, of course."

"What are we going to do with her?"

"We'll let her graze in the grassy field near to the house at first, then she'll go to the new paddock you've been clearing, when it's had time to mature."

She seemed at home with us, as she immediately began to strip the grass. After a while, she got down on her knees and settled on the ground to chew her cud, and I lay on her plump, warm tummy in the sunshine. I know she liked me because she nuzzled me, and licked me with her rough tongue. I named her Betsy.

I was to be responsible, along with my two elder brothers, for feeding and milking, before and after school. Dad taught us how to milk her, as he had learned from Peppa as a lad, but I couldn't seem to grasp the hang of it as well as Jim and John did, who both went at it like threshing machines.

♪ ♫ ♪ ♫ ♪

One early morning in 1949, bucket at the ready, I made my way to the cowshed, with nothing on my mind other than the job in hand.

I placed Betsy's fodder in the manger and, because she fidgeted so fretfully against my clumsy efforts at milking her, I tied her leg back as usual. Then I settled down on the small stool, singing away as usual while

I Remember Me

I attempted, yet again, to extract the last drop for the breakfast table. Then suddenly... well! She was as astounded as I was, because she stopped her feeding, let out a deep, vibrating grunt and jerked her head around. . Her big baleful eyes met my own startled gape.

Coming to my senses, I rushed from the shed and shot across the yard to the kitchen. The bucket clanked in my hand as I fled, while milk sloshed over its brim, leaving a trail of white droplets behind me like pearls in the dust. I burst through the kitchen door, trapping my long-suffering Mum behind the sink.

"What the Dickens!" was all she could exclaim, before I interrupted.

"Mum! Mum! Just listen to this!"

She gave a quizzical, sideways sort of a look, as if to say "What now?" But she stopped what she was doing, dried her hands, and waited.

I took a deep breath, uttered a silent prayer that it would happen again, then I launched into it. The kitchen walls echoed to the sound, sending back to my ears the ringing falsetto tones of... my very own fully-fledged yodel.

Betsy, our cow

Mum stood, bemused, in stunned silence, then a grin emerged onto her lips and slowly spread across her face.

"Well, what do you think?" I demanded, breathlessly.

She gave me quick hug, the way mums do, especially when you're feeling all grown up and would much rather they didn't. The matter in hand was far too important for all that. Then she held me at arm's length, a hand on each shoulder, and looked me straight in the eyes.

"I'm impressed, Frank," she said, "and truly amazed!"

She went on to confess she had always had a fancy to yodel, and she could only think her desire had imprinted itself homogeneously upon my chromosomes.

It was my turn to be amazed. To think, I'd never known that before. I looked at her closely and I had to admit I did resemble her facially; but to have inherited her desire to yodel? That seemed farfetched. One thing neither parent could do was hold down a tune, let alone a yodel. We've had many happy times spent round the piano with Mum playing the accompaniment while we all suffered Dad's rendition of *Abdul Abulbul*

Amir. Although I loved the song, I have to say Dad's version of it bore little resemblance to the actual melody.

No, the true source of my yodel was in the music I listened to on the radio and the artists I tried to emulate. Yodelling was an inherent part of this music and I naturally made an attempt to yodel myself. It developed quite spontaneously, so the event was as much a surprise to me, as it was to Mum.

I remember becoming aware of the yodel while listening to Gran's favourite singer from the thirties, Smoky Dawson. Smoky had a regular radio show and sometimes I would sit with Gran to listen, because I liked to hear his adventures with his horse Flash. Smoky would sing on the show and often burst into a yodel, which my Gran seemed to enjoy immensely.

My inspiration also came from the many Hillbilly programmes that abounded on Australian country radio stations in those days. As in England, with Big Bill Campbell, it was the Canadians who seemed to dominate this field, more than their American counterparts. The most significant of these were Wilf Carter and Hank Snow. However, Wilf Carter was probably the most influential foreign country music entertainer of the time, leaving an indelible imprint on many Australian country singers, and his songs are still performed today. Hank Snow went on to become legendary both in Australia and in the United States, where he was a regular host on Radio WSM's *Grand Ole Opry*.

Three other Canadians of that period who spring to mind are Bob Dyer, Smiling Billy Blinkhorne and Orval Prophet. So impressed was I with Orval's style that I was to record no less than three of his songs *Going Back To Birmingham*, *Little Band Of Gold* and the lovely *Molly Darling* I first heard my Grandpa sing.

Of the contemporary American performers, Jimmie Rodgers and Hank Williams figured prominently, followed by the Hollywood cowboy stars, Gene Autry, Roy Rodgers and The Sons Of The Pioneers. Then there were the firmly established local artists, like Tex Morton, Buddy Williams and Slim Dusty. Of these few home-grown products, I most admired Tex. He was actually from New Zealand and was a great showman who toured Australia with his storytelling country songs. Buddy Williams, too, carved his name in Australian history as a singing pioneer who managed to encapsulate the essence of Australia in his music. However, Slim Dusty has the greatest longevity as the uncrowned king of Australian country music, known here and overseas for his giant hit *A Pub With No Beer*.

I Remember Me

Even so, despite all these influences, it is really through Peppa I inherited my love of singing, and it is due to my Gran that I discovered my yodel - and it all began in the cow shed.

♪ ♫ ♪ ♫ ♪

Now I had found my yodel, I had a burning ambition to perfect it, even though it meant hours of practice. It impressed Betsy - not that she was given much choice. However, I began to notice the falsetto seemed somehow to sedate her and she didn't struggle or fidget in the way she used to. Furthermore, I appeared to be getting a higher yield of milk as a result. This was a discovery I made for myself, yet subsequently I was to learn that yodelling was practised the world over for the precise purpose of calming herds of goats, sheep, and cattle.

The problem of the guitar was partially solved, when, for my eleventh birthday, Mum and Dad bought me a ukulele. All right, so it wasn't a guitar, but it was a start. Assiduously, I studied the little diagrams over the songs on the sheet music and learned how to finger the chords. Now, in the quiet of my bedroom, I could accompany myself as I sang. Slowly but surely I was becoming a budding, self-contained, music man.

My brother John and I would often harmonise together and he tried, without too much success, to yodel in harmony while he played the banjo-mandolin and I played my ukulele. Jim attempted the accordion, Robert played bass and all the family tried, and quickly gave up, on the fiddle.

Mum and Gran were both supportive of my singing and would take the time and trouble to listen to my songs. I often cursed over the inadequacies of my ukulele and expressed how I longed for a proper acoustic guitar so I could accompany myself like the singers on the radio. Gran said nothing to me but, week by week, she put aside a little money from her war widow's pension. Then one day, after I'd regaled her with yet another impromptu performance, she unexpectedly asked:

"Is it a real guitar you'd be wanting Frank?"

Was it ever? She didn't need an answer - she could see the desire emblazoned all over my face.

She smiled her gentle smile, placed her careworn hand on mine, and squeezed it until I could feel the imprint of her ring hard against my flesh.

"Happen you shall have one for Christmas, then!" she declared. "But first you must promise to persevere and learn to play it just as diligently as you have th'ukulele."

It All Began in a Cowshed

"Oh, I will!" I promised, knowing full well I would have no difficulty in keeping that promise - it was what I wanted most in all the world.

We journeyed together to a music shop in Bligh Street, Sydney, to choose my first guitar. The shop was a veritable treasure trove of musical instruments of all shapes and sizes, and one wall was entirely devoted to rows of shiny new guitars. I walked up and down, rapt in awe at this wondrous spectacle, but there was one 'flat top' that took my eye time and time again. It was black with green palm trees, and it stood there, demanding me to play it.

"That one," I said, and I gazed steadfastly at it, my tongue flicking across my lips in anticipation, while it was taken down and placed in my hands. My fingers found a chord and its mellow tone was the sweetest sound I had ever heard. I walked from the shop, head held high in the knowledge that, come Christmas, I would be the proud owner of a professional guitar.

Even now, I only need to think of it and the distinctive aroma of my prized possession comes floating back. I named it 'Bessie' in honour of my Gran. At the time I had no inkling of the sacrifice it must have been for her to part with such a large sum from her small savings, and I shall remain ever grateful to her for the faith she showed in me.

Now I had my guitar, it was rarely out of my hands. Indeed, it frequently accompanied me to school, only now I had to go by bus for fear of scratching it on branches or barbed wire fences. I practised in the schoolyard, and gradually found I was attracting the attention of my fellow pupils.

My stance among them grew, and I began to taste again that sense of power I had experienced all those years ago in front of my classmates in the air raid shelter - the power to hold an audience. My headmaster, Mr. Bates, also began to take notice of my music. To encourage me, he would select a piece of Australian poetry, ask me to make up my own tune and guitar accompaniment to it, and then he would ask me to perform the song in front of the class. It was through Mr Bates's evident passion for these historical pioneer verses that I, too, was developing a love of traditional Australian ballads and I simply burst with pride when he asked me to sing one of them in the forthcoming school production at the Dural Memorial Hall. I selected my song and practised hard.

Finally, the big day came. Through the draped bed linen hanging as a screen between the hall and the stage, I managed to sneak a peek at the audience as they drifted in. I felt a secret thrill of pride pass through me when I spotted our Mum, Dad and Gran walking down to their seats near

I Remember Me

the front, with little Philip in tow, his thumb stuck in his mouth and his big round eyes taking in the strangeness of his surroundings.

The racket of voices calmed to a murmur when Mr. Bates walked onto the stage to welcome the parents and citizens. Then the show opened. I enjoyed the play-acting, where in cap and gown I launched myself into my role as a Headmaster in a little sketch. Somehow, my performance seemed magically boosted by the application of makeup, the donning of a costume, and the reaction of a live audience. Robert's class, with their pirate song, went over well, and I followed this with a silly poem about a mouse, which only got a half-hearted response - but what did that matter? I was saving myself for the pièce-de-resistance, my solo singing spot.

Dressed in my best suit, hair slicked back and tidy, I felt strangely vulnerable while my guitar and I waited to be announced, and I offered a silent prayer all would go as rehearsed. Then the sheet was yanked aside, exposing me to the critical inspection of the outside world. I walked briskly and determinedly to the centre stage, conscious of an expectant mass waiting in the dimmed house lights - waiting for ME. I took a deep breath, gained my composure, and looked them straight in the eye. My fingers just itched to do my bidding as my guitar brought forth its first familiar chord - and I was away. Amazingly, I sang and played with no mistakes, and my song soon came to the last stanza...

> *...I've seen a bullock stretch and strain and blink its bleary eye,*
> *Where the dog sits on the tucker box, nine miles from Gundagai.*

I bowed in response to the resounding round of applause that seemed to go on for ever, then stood with a satisfied smile, nodding my appreciation into the lights, wondering what on earth I should be doing next. In the end I mouthed "thank-you" and went off with the warmth of the reception following me into the wings. I was walking on air, filled with an exhilaration the likes of which I'd never known before.

An ambition was born that day, an affirmation that this was what I wanted to do for the rest of my life. The problem was, though, how was I to embark on a career in music? Apart from the Dural Memorial Hall, where else could I perform? Although I loved the bush, I began to realise the limitations of my home there as a base from which to launch my dreams.

That wasn't my only problem. I was growing rapidly and at age twelve I was tall beyond my years. I towered over all my classmates, including 'Sir', earning myself the nickname 'Lanky Frankie'. In fact, I was literally growing too big for my britches.

I was beginning to notice the girls in the class were growing, too, and one young lady in particular had acquired a pair of tastily rounded protuberances. My surreptitious glances her way resulted in a strange stirring of the loins, making it hard to leap to my feet without causing myself an injury. Such was the case one day when I was called to front the class to read an essay. All heads turned to watch as I rose, red-faced and bent over like a banana, while my hot blood battled with the brevity of my shorts.

However, I was forced to wait until my thirteenth birthday for my first pair of long trousers. Beige they were, with a razor edge crease, a vision of sartorial elegance, and I sighed with relief. I looked and felt fantastic - a popinjay in a pair of long pants.

But I hadn't just grown out of my shorts; I'd outgrown the little Dural primary school too. John and Jim had long been at high school, but there were no places available for me, so I'd had to stay where I was.

Meanwhile, Dad's little corner of the Lucas empire was growing, too, which meant Lucas Laboratories were about to commandeer our bedrooms. A decision was taken that would both evacuate us from the factory premises and facilitate the furtherance of my education: we were about to grub stakes and move house once more.

-6-

ROLL UP - ROLL UP

I have to admit, my parents were right - the opportunity to broaden my education was indeed much greater when I moved to Carlingford High School. But I doubt the schooling they envisaged for their son was quite the same as he was undergoing now at his desk - where 'spellbound' had replaced 'spelling' in his timetable.

To come straight from a cosy country primary school into this hotbed of academic excellence was hard to cope with. It was an unfortunate time to join, halfway through the last term of the year, especially since I had so much to catch up on. The teachers were patient, however, and allowed me to settle in at my own pace and feel my own way for the remainder of the term.

The curriculum was much wider and offered new and interesting subjects, my favourites being the hands-on metalwork, carpentry and technical drawing classes that required some artistic skills and creativity. Science and technology I found stimulating, too. But mathematics - that was always my Achilles heel. I'd had difficulty when the subject was known as sums, even more when it became arithmetic and now, suddenly, here I was confronted by a class delving into the realms of logarithms, algebra and the like.

I found my mind going walkabout. My eyes would slide wistfully over the studious concentration of my fellow classmates until they lighted upon the perfectly sculptured face of Jeanette. Never mind mathematics, it was her I would study assiduously, weighing her up from every angle as an artist would when painting a portrait - her hair, fashioned just above shoulder length, her expressive eyes, her delicate retroussé nose - until her image became imprinted upon my soul.

This image was unleashed at night to haunt me. She would silently slip into my dreams, wearing nothing but a look of desire to which I could offer no resistance. I simply had to surrender and abandon myself to wild erotic fantasies. But then, in the cold light of day, how different everything was; how difficult it all became. If she happened a glance in my direction I would quickly turn away to hide my blushes.

Yes, I was grappling with the first pangs of puppy love, pangs so painful that they would tear me asunder - yet somehow the agony was strangely exhilarating; the thrilling sensation of pure self torture.

Roll Up – Roll Up

In the desk next to mine sat my mate Michael. We both showed a penchant for woodworking and planned a carpentry business together when we left school. We were best mates and to him I opened my heart.

Four o'clock one Friday, we were waiting together for the school bus. I was paying no attention to Michael for, as usual, my lovesick eyes were riveted on the distant object of my affection. Suddenly I spotted him, swaggering right up to her. I saw her oval eyes open wide at his approach and focus full on his face and I was gripped with an unspeakable envy.

If this were just a simple case of the faint heart never winning fair maiden, I could accept my lot, but this was treachery, a betrayal of my trust by him I called my mate. When he came back and boasted that he had asked her out to the picture theatre at Castle Hill, I glared my fury at him. He laughed - a taunting laugh that hovered in the charged air between us. A flash of red rage crashed through my brain and before I knew it, my arm was locked around his neck. With one almighty twist he crumpled to the ground. I was on him in an instant, lashing out at him as our two bodies landed heavily together, rolling in the dust. The skirmish was sudden and savage and was being egged on like a dog fight by the kids who had now formed a circle around us. Two irate teachers came pushing through.

"What the bloody hell's going on here then?" one of them demanded as he grabbed my arm and pulled me off.

I rose up without a word and walked away, nursing my cuts and bruises, but able to hold my head up proudly once more. Although I was not entirely cured of Cupid's sting, time would no doubt heal my yearning for her. But as for Michael, well, the affair marked the end of any future joint company aspirations.

♪ ♫ ♪ ♫ ♪

Our new home was in the northern suburbs of Sydney at 95 Copeland Road, Beecroft, in the leafy Hills District. Dad and Mum, once again, had made the right choice - a large, authentic Colonial style house exuding charm and character that was to become the Ifield family seat for the following thirty odd years. Beecroft would have to rank as one of the most beautiful villages in the suburbs of Sydney. In spring its charm is enhanced by the riot of colour in every garden and the evening air is sweetly intoxicating with the perfume of magnolia and frangipani blossom.

I Remember Me

But how I missed the solace of the bush. To be parted from its therapeutic influence felt like I'd had a vital limb amputated. So accustomed was I to opening the door and rushing into the bosom of unbridled nature, the paths meandering between manicured gardens outside our new abode seemed a sterile substitute by comparison.

I took consolation in my music. Where before I had sung my heart out to the wide wilderness, now I shut myself away. In the privacy of the bathroom, I could be heard perpetually practising - picking and strumming on my guitar while the reverberation off its tiled walls enhanced the sound of my trills. I'd play my records over and over or I'd be glued to the radio, listening avidly to a wide selection of all kinds of music, learning, dissecting and analysing. My taste was maturing and I was discovering jazz, finding I had a fondness for singers such as Brook Benton, Dinah Washington, Sarah Vaughn, Nat King Cole and the great musicians of the time like Quincy Jones, Louis Armstrong, Stan Getz and Paul Mulligan. With my teens had come the advent of the fifties and the pop singers who were also to make their mark on me, like the great Frankie Laine, Guy Mitchell and Johnny Ray.

I found a soul-mate in my brother John, who would often join in with my singing, and we rehearsed so much that at times we even spoke in harmony. We perfected a duet of a song popular at the time, *They Cut Down The Old Pine Tree*, recorded by the Legarde Twins. Inspired by an advert in the local paper, I inveigled John into coming with me to cut a two-bit private recording of the song. We ended up recording in a converted garage and, need I say, it was no technical masterpiece. For one thing, the 78 rpm disc was cut from the centre out, making it nigh impossible to play. However, it did serve to fire my aspirations even further and I was getting desperate to find an outlet for them.

♪♫♪♫♪

With a gruelling school term behind us, John and I were in the mood for letting off steam. Our local county fair, the Castle Hill Show, was a major event in the Easter calendar, proudly boasted as being second only to Sydney's famous Royal Easter Show. We decided to go.

Mingling with the masses around the side-shows, we tried our hand at the duck shoot, hoop-la and coconut shy, and came to a halt outside Jimmie Sharman's Boxing tent where a contestant was being drummed up from the crowd.

Roll Up – Roll Up

However, my attention was on the next tent, captured by the splendid figure of a North American Red Indian dressed in full regalia: buckskins, moccasins, turquoise beads and a magnificent full-feathered chieftain's head-dress. In language as colourful as his costume, he was hurling insults in the direction of the neighbouring marquee, from where they were being returned like a boomerang, with equal force. I recognised his adversaries as Tom and Ted Legarde, the same Legarde Twins whose song John and I had recorded.

I took John's arm and we joined the crowd, listening to the people taking sides as the feud hardened. I gathered that, for some reason, the Red Indian had just dispensed with the Twins' services as his supporting act and, in retaliation, they had set up their own show. Incensed by their effrontery, the Chief threw out a challenge that made my ears prick up.

"I could take someone out of the crowd right now and make them a bigger star act than you will ever be."

I jabbed John in the ribs and blurted out, "Come on John, let's volunteer!"

"No, not me Frank - but why don't you?"

"OK," I said, and shouted at the top of my lungs, "Hey, how about me? I'll have a go!"

"Good on you," bellowed the Chief. "Come to the back of the tent and we'll show these good people I mean what I say."

I seized the moment and hurried to the rear of the marquee. There he was, waiting, and although I was a tall, strapping lad for my thirteen years, I felt small in the presence of this larger-than-life figure. He was none other than Big Chief Little Wolf, the wrestler, famed throughout Australia for his Indian Death Lock. He lifted his forearm, palm outward, and rumbled a deep 'How!' at me, just as they do in the movies.

"What's your name and what sort of singer are you, son?"

"I sing Country and Western, sir, and my name is Frank Ifield."

"That's perfect. Then you play guitar too, don't you Frank?"

"Yes sir, but I've left mine at home."

"Don't worry. Here, you can use mine," he said as he thrust a Gibson flat top into my hands. "I want you ready to start in five minutes sharp."

With that, he turned on his moccasins and strutted like a gladiator to the middle of the ring, leaving me no chance to argue - even if I'd wanted to. Five minutes went by so fast but I was prepared and ready when the Chief delivered his introduction.

I Remember Me

"And now, Ladies and gentlemen, you're in for a big treat. Here to sing for us today is a wonderful new talent. May I present your own, your very own, local rising young star - Frank Ifield."

I sprang into action, bounding across the sawdust like a demented kangaroo until I reached the centre, where I immediately launched into *Oh Boy, How She Could Yodel*. The audience was the same crowd who, only minutes before, had heard me volunteer my services. They were willing me to do well, for they met my bow with enthusiastic clapping and cheering.

"Thank you," I said, and tentatively started my exit - but Little Wolf blocked it.

"Not so fast, young fella," he said, flashing his teeth at me. "Go and sing another."

I turned to face the audience again, frantically searching in my mind for the right song. The sight of John, beaming from the front row, inspired me and I started into our favourite Hank Snow song, *Broken Dreams*. Then, without pause, I went for the grand slam with *Big Rock Candy Mountain*.

I took my leave, bathing in the applause and glancing at the Chief, hoping he was impressed. Impressed? I'll say he was. As we passed one another, we exchanged grins and he held my arm up like a champion. "I'll see you later," he whispered.

I watched his act in a daze, wondering what he had in mind. A gift, a thank-you token maybe?

"How would you like to tour with me this summer?"

He interpreted my look of blank disbelief as needing further persuasion.

"It'll be good experience for an aspiring young man - and I'll give you a pound a day, plus expenses."

"Er..." I stuttered.

"Just one thing. You'll need a stage outfit - Western style, with a hat."

Then he handed me his card. I stowed it carefully in my pocket as if it were made of pure gold. In our excitement, John and I giggled all the way home.

The very second we walked through the door, we cornered Mum and poured out a jumbled account of all that had occurred.

"Oh Mum," I tried to convince her, "just think, I could be just like Grandpa Peppa, touring in a travelling show."

Mum pondered a while, for she understood just how gullible and impetuous her son was. It seemed a long time before she took the Chief's card in her hand and went to the phone.

She replaced the receiver, stood for a moment in thoughtful hesitation, then looking into my eager face, she said, "All right, as long as it's only for the school holidays."

I must confess to being quite gratified by my reflection in the shop mirror as I tried on a black stage outfit. Both the long sleeved black shirt and the trousers had gold corded edging, and I saw atop my smiling face the crowning glory - a large black Stetson to match. "A proper cowboy!" I thought as I dug deep into my savings to become their proud possessor.

Summer came at last and, armed with my baggage and guitar, I arrived at Parramatta railway station where Big Chief Little Wolf met me in a large American Cadillac limousine. During our long journey to Wagga Wagga, he explained what was required of me. I was to help in cajoling the crowd to roll up for the show by 'spruiking' as he called it. First, I would sell myself to the crowd, after which he would join me. Once they'd been coaxed into buying tickets, I was to hasten into the marquee and start the show. After my act, I would introduce him. Then, at the conclusion of the show, I would return to the front of the tent to spruik again for the next show. So it would continue, turn and turn about, for around a dozen shows throughout the day.

The minute we arrived, I had to assist in setting up the marquee. Nobody showed me what to do, I just mucked in to learn the ropes, so to speak, as I went along. Soon we were ready for our first performance.

It was early morning and there were only a few people milling around as I climbed the ladder onto the raised wooden platform over the entrance of the marquee. I'd never had to blow my own trumpet before, so I felt very self-conscious as I took a deep breath, lifted the megaphone and demanded:

"Roll up! - Roll up!"

No one so much as turned a hair. I would have to do better than that if we were to fill the tent. There was nothing for it but to burble on...

"Inside the big marquee, now starring the world famous Red Indian wrestler, who will demonstrate his famous Indian death-lock. Ladies and gentlemen, I give you - Big Chief Little Wolf."

Thankfully, the Chief climbed the platform and, with his professional expertise, he soon had a crowd gathering around. Then he handed back to me, saying "Tell them about yourself son."

I Remember Me

"Well," I started tentatively, "My name's Frank Ifield, and I hail from the hills of Cumberland County. Inside the tent today, you will hear me sing your special requests - yes, your favourite Country and Western songs."

This announcement inspired not a murmur from the crowd. A new and braver tack was needed...

"Come on you miserable lot over there - yes, you mate! Bring your friends closer. Come and join us as we sing some of your favourites like, 'Get out of the cornfield Nellie, we're going against the grain'."

Somehow, this grabbed their attention. Why, even the Chief gave a mini ha-ha behind my back. Then I let rip with a rebel yell, "Wee-haa!" and that really got 'em. "Now we're cooking! I've got your favourite song here sir, 'South Of The Border'. Yes, my girl lived south of the border, too, but last night, she came across!"

I had learned a few of these silly lines while watching comedians in variety shows and now they were coming in handy. I found the crowds liked a bit of cheek and the singling out of individuals, yet I suspect I got away with a lot because of my youth.

In my infrequent breaks, I liked to wander around the show-ground to view the other attractions. However, it was no fun always having to parade around dressed like Roy Rodgers. I stood out like a shag on a rock, which invited yahoo's, and jibes of 'ride 'em cowboy' and, after enduring a few days of this, I decided to protest.

"Do I always have to wear this outfit, Chief?" I dared to ask. "It attracts attention and it's embarrassing."

"Attracts attention?" he laughed. "Of course it attracts attention! You want to be in show business, don't you kid?"

"Yes, sir," I affirmed sheepishly.

"Well then, what are you whinging about? Get back out there and SHOW!"

And of course, he was right. By causing people to talk and take notice, I was a walking advertisement for the show. Why, the Chief himself took every opportunity to dress up in his ceremonial costume and, indeed, he amazed me on many occasions. Even when just pulling up for petrol, he'd don his head-dress before roaring up to the petrol-bowser in a flourish of feathers.

In the face of this solid logic, I took my pride in hand, went back out as he ordered and braved it. I remembered what my dad used to say - "Nobody can make you feel inferior son, without your permission" - and it suddenly came to me what he meant: I had to face my complexes in order to conquer them. I've always remembered this incident and must admit it helped to strengthen my bravado for future shows.

We travelled far and wide to appear wherever a carnival, agricultural show, rodeo or gymkhana was being held. Once we had erected the tent, the Chief would arrange our accommodation, which would be either at the local pub, dossing down in an on-site caravan or sometimes in the tent itself.

This was the first time this little eagle had flown the nest and I longed for the comfort of the family tree. I was so busy in the day there was no time to brood, but at night I'd find myself laying awake, thinking of home. I missed my mum and I knew she'd be worrying about me so, in my few idle moments, I comforted myself by composing this little song for her.

I am leaving the homestead today Mum,
Dry your eyes and give me one last smile;
I am leaving the friends all behind me,
I'll think of you while I trudge every mile.
Your smile will live on in my memory,
Like a rose that's been kissed by the dew,
Let your eyes sparkle bright,
For they guide me through the night,
Keep smiling though you may feel blue.
[A Mothers Faith]

Working with the Chief was an honour and a privilege and he taught this enthusiastic greenhorn a lot about showbusiness and presentation. He was a loveable eccentric, with a big heart and a friendly smile for everyone. His famous Indian Death Lock was a wrestling hold from which there was no escape - and believe me, I know, because he'd frequently demonstrate on me when he couldn't get a volunteer from the audience. Yet, no matter how hard I practised it on my brothers, I never could master it.

As promised, I returned home in time for school, though settling back into its humdrum routine was doubly difficult after the excitement of my first touring show. It's true, I hadn't been paid a fortune, but the wealth of experience I had gained was valuable beyond belief.

I Remember Me

A proper cowboy. My first stage outfit, complete with stetson, and my first guitar, Bessie, that my gran had bought for me.

-7-
LITTLE WHITE LIES

He'd cast such a spell over me, I didn't know quite what to expect, and when the man himself emerged from his dressing room, I watched, mesmerised, as he signed books and various bits of scrap paper. When my turn came, I gratefully accepted his autograph and floated off in a dream, having completely forgotten the original intention of my mission.

I'd gone to see Country and Western star Tim McNamara performing in his own show at Eastwood Theatre, and he made a big impression on me as a fine performer, whose gentle style came wafting across the footlights. As I watched, it struck me that I should be in his show. Determined to seek him out, I'd ventured back stage, and found myself standing in line with his fans.

I was so annoyed with myself for having flunked my first approach that, when I went to see him again at The Hornsby Pacific Cabaret, I resolved not to be distanced by him. Full of bravado, I went backstage before the show, marched straight up to him and asked for an audition. To put it politely, he made it known quite bluntly he was far too busy to be bothered. In that one moment, my idol had shattered his image and it lay in shreds around my feet. But I wasn't going to be put off.

Instead, it was his brother Tommy Mack, the show's compère and comedian, who now fell victim. Tommy obligingly found time to listen to me sing and liked what he heard. In fact, he was so keen he insisted I remain backstage.

I watched, fascinated, as act followed act until Tommy introduced somebody who missed their cue. We waited. The audience waited. Tommy told another joke and waited. Still no one appeared. It was my time and I knew it. I was already poised in the wings with my guitar in the play-me position when Tommy announced me.

I entered the stage to a polite flutter of hands and lunged into a Hank Snow favourite of mine, *Golden Rocket*. This song is always a tongue twister at the best of times and, in my over-enthusiastic haste, I rattled through it at double tempo. The bewildered audience dutifully applauded, even though I doubt they understood one word of it.

Calmed by their acceptance, I went into my next song and was in full flow when, out of the corner of my eye, I spied a sinister silhouette in the wings, wildly waving its arms about. It dawned on me that this was Tim

I Remember Me

himself, signalling me to get off - but my audience was now clapping warmly, insisting on an encore. I weighed the odds, decided they were in my favour and stayed where I was. After a few more encores, I took my curtain calls and swiftly exited, on the opposite side to Tim.

It transpired he was, albeit begrudgingly, impressed, and signed me up for more shows at the meagre fee of one pound and one shilling per concert. I'd done it. My first professional engagement on the theatre stage.

The next time I appeared in Hornsby, it was as a fully-fledged member of Tim's show. I might not have been earning a princely sum in return for my services, but I was receiving invaluable experience in presenting myself to theatre audiences. Taking this one step further, I decided to conduct an experiment, just to see how far I could go in projecting myself from the stage. I nearly took it too far.

During my days at Dural school, watching Headmaster Bates as he presented his subject to the class, I'd noticed that whenever he was passionately interested in what he was teaching, he would appear larger than life in front of my eyes. On the other hand, if the subject were one for which he himself cared little, he would seem to shrink smaller and smaller until he became so insignificant that I was totally oblivious of his presence at all.

Using this analogy as the basis of my experiment, I determined to sing only the songs I felt passionate about, in order to project myself larger than life across the footlights. This evening, at Hornsby, I decided to put my theory into practice. It seemed to be proving valid: the stronger I focused on putting my soul into the delivery of my songs, the more I seemed to enter the very heart of each individual in my audience. My concentration heightened to a peak of intensity during the dramatic theme song from the motion picture High Noon, and I took off - literally. One moment I was singing, the next I was floating at the rear of the theatre from where I could clearly see myself performing on the stage. I drifted in this state of disembodiment for some time until, suddenly, the illusion shattered and I was back to reality. I tried to continue with the song, but the experience made me not only lose my words, but even forget what song I was singing.

The experiment had worked - but worked too well. I'd conjured up an out-of-body experience and frightened the life out of myself. The basic principle was right, but I decided I'd be more careful how I applied it in future.

♪♫♪♫♪

Little White Lies

In those pre-television days, live shows of all descriptions were plentiful and popular with the Australian public. One form of entertainment enjoyed by many was the talent contest. Although I was already performing professionally with Tim, in my incessant quest for further recognition, I entered as many of the better ones as possible. One venue in particular was the regular Sunday evening open air concert at Eden Park in North Ryde. To encourage a packed audience, they would book professional star artistes, with the talent contest as a cheap supporting attraction.

Often seen topping the bill was the popular yodeller, Lily Connors. Gosh, was she a stunner. One look at her and my legs turned to jelly. No wonder her mother always came with her for protection against moonstruck lads like me. As she swayed across the stage in her short, fringed skirt and high heeled riding boots the audience could be heard to sigh "Oh, boy, can she sing!" My mind boggled at the thought of how we two yodellers could have made sweet music together. Yet we were poles apart; she was an already established recording artiste whereas I was a mere fourteen-year-old starry-eyed hopeful.

One Sunday, I persuaded our John to enter the contest with me. All the singing and rehearsing we did together certainly paid dividends - we won first prize. Gaining in confidence, I began to enter solo and, spurred on by a growing following of fans, I won on several occasions over the next few months.

However, I had my sights set higher. Headliners at Eden Park were invariably kind and helpful, and Country Music recording stars, Rick and Thel Carey, were no exception. They seemed to take a particular interest in me, so I decided to ask them how I could set about making a record.

"First of all, you need some original songs," they advised.

Their guidance was obviously sound, but the only original songs I had were my own compositions. How did the likes of me find brand-new professional material? They had the answer.

"Make an appointment to see Allan Crawford, manager of Southern Music in Sydney. He's a personal friend of ours."

Well, that sounded easy enough. Of course it would mean skipping school for a day - still, the way I saw it, my career depended on it. Unfortunately, I couldn't follow the Carey's advice completely, because there was no way I could arrange an appointment to see this Mr Crawford. I could only bunk off school when the opportunity presented itself. I couldn't see that it would make much difference if I just turned up.

I Remember Me

So one October morning in 1952, this eager, young fourteen-year-old novice with guitar in hand, swaggered, completely unheralded, into the offices of the Southern Music Publishing Company, Sydney. Brazenly, I strutted up to the reception desk, where I requested audience with Mr Crawford. Overhearing me, a man with a big toothy smile emerged from his segregated office box and enquired who I was and how he might help. I went into my previously rehearsed speech.

"I'm Frank Ifield, a friend of Rick and Thel Carey. They have recommended I see Mr Crawford with a view to obtaining some new and original songs."

"I am Allan Crawford," he replied and went on to explain, somewhat sharply I thought, "We can't hand out songs, willy-nilly, to anyone who walks in off the street. Artists have to be assigned to a recording company, or at least be well known on radio, before we can consider material for them."

At that he turned to go, intimating an end to the interview.

I wasn't prepared to accept a rebuff; I'd come too far to be put off quite so readily. There was nothing for it - I had to act, and act quickly. In the nick of time, just as he was about to disappear, I threw in a great big whopper...

"I have a recording session coming up shortly," I bluffed, praying God would forgive me.

It worked. He stopped in his tracks and when he turned to face me again, there was a smile on his lips, and his tone of voice changed completely.

"Well, that's a different matter. Who with?"

In a panic, I quickly scanned through my memory banks, visualising the labels on my favourite discs, and pulled one out of the hat.

"Regal Zonophone" I stated emphatically.

"Oh," he nodded in approval, "that's EMI."

I could see he was impressed, and I felt a resurgence of confidence. It was short-lived. Turning to his secretary, he said "Get Ron Wills of EMI on the phone would you please?"

Icy terror tingled up and down my spine, and my hair stood on end, prickling the back of my neck. My ruse was about to backfire, and there was nothing I could do about it. I was just eyeing the doorway, ready to make a run for it, when fate intervened.

"Mr Wills is out and won't be back until after lunch. Do you want to leave a message?" announced the secretary. I gave her a half-crazed grin in my relief, then turned my eyes onto Allan Crawford, willing his reply, which he duly issued.

"Oh no, don't worry," he said, glancing at his watch, "I'll have to phone him later. I have a lunch appointment, too."

He gave me a wry smile, which told me that he didn't quite believe me, but I'd got away with it for now. Aloud, he said, "I'll speak to Ron Wills later this afternoon. Meanwhile, I'll let you hear some of our latest releases from the States, but you mustn't take any records away with you. My secretary will be here to assist you."

I stumbled over some words of thanks, then he bade me farewell and I watched him disappear through the door. His secretary took me into the listening room and sifted through a pile of records, sorting some suitable songs for me to hear. As soon as she'd gone, I got down to work. There was a lot to do, and so little time. I selected a song and settled down to listen. The music started. The sentiment was heartrending, but the tune was melodic and quite simple to learn. Fortunately, I found it easy to commit a song quickly to memory and, after playing it over maybe three times, I had it mastered, guitar chords and all. Time to go. I left behind a smile of appreciation with Allan Crawford's secretary as I departed, acutely aware of her bewilderment at my hasty retreat.

Allan Crawford, the man I bluffed into giving me my chance for a recording contract.

I was off to track down Ron Wills. I had to confront him before Allan Crawford had a chance to speak to him, to prevent any sabotage to my plan. The problem was, EMI offices were in Homebush, and that was a thirty-minute train journey away. I managed to elbow my way through the sauntering lunchtime crowds, and raced to catch the train as if the hounds of doom were on my tail.

I Remember Me

Lady Luck was still by my side, and I arrived just as the train pulled in. Through the window, buildings whizzed by as if my whole life were flashing before me. Finally, we slowed into Homebush station and I caught sight of the EMI sign. The brisk trot to the Parramatta Road had me gasping for breath, and I had to stop for a moment to regain my composure. I straightened my clothes, patted my hair into place, wiped the sweat from my brow and hoped that my red face would be attributed the midday heat. Scared stiff, but as ready as I'd ever be, I entered the offices of EMI.

At the main desk, I asked the receptionist for Mr Wills. She replied that he was at lunch, which was just what I had hoped to hear.

"Do you have an appointment?" she went on to ask.

"N-No," I stammered, "but I need to see him urgently. It won't take a moment. Perhaps I could see him when he arrives back..."

She gave me a pitying look.

"All right then. You'd better take a seat and wait. He shouldn't be too long."

She indicated a row of chairs against the wall, then went back to her work.

"Thank you," I said, but I realised I had another problem - I didn't know what he looked like. I hovered, wondering how to ask.

She must have sensed my anxiety, for she looked up again and smiled. It was a kindly smile so, with all the charm this callow youth could muster, I explained I hadn't met Mr Wills before, and asked if she would please point him out to me as he returned. She very kindly acquiesced - to my utter relief.

I sat down to wait and, eventually, a man came in through the door. He was tall, well over six-foot, yet with his gentle smile and kind eyes he seemed an approachable sort of gentleman and I hoped it was Mr. Wills. I looked at the receptionist. She looked my way and winked. Yes, it was indeed the man in question.

This was my big moment. I took a deep breath, walked forward and said "Excuse me Mr. Wills, I know we haven't met before, but my name's Frank Ifield, and I've come to see you at Allan Crawford's recommendation with a view to recording. Maybe you could just spare a moment or two to hear me sing one of his published songs?"

He was a little taken aback, but I floundered on. "I've just now come over from Southern Music, where I've been given a new song from the States... it really won't take long..."

My self-assurance was fading fast, but just as I was frantically searching for further persuasive words, he yielded.

"Oh, all right then," he said, "but it had better be quick. I'm a busy man." I can only suppose he thought it would be the quickest way of getting rid of me. He ushered me to a listening booth where I launched, full tilt, into the newly acquired song.

He looked pleasantly surprised when I'd finished. "Hmm. That sounds good. I like the way you sing. But, as you must know, exposure is of paramount importance before even considering a recording contract." He regarded me thoughtfully. "Are you touring at the moment, or doing a radio series?"

Quick Frank, think, I told myself. Another white lie won't hurt... you're in it good and deep now... OK, here goes...

"I'm about to be on Radio 2GB for *Australia's Amateur Hour*."

"Oh! When will that be?"

Oh no, what could I say now...?

"They haven't set the date yet," I chanced. I could see he wasn't fully convinced so I continued, "I'll phone you this afternoon to confirm it."

"Fine," he said as he quickly disappeared into his office. I stared after him, in utter disbelief at my own audacity.

I left EMI on a high. In contrast to the outward journey, the ride back to the city was a welcome respite while I unwound a little. I got to town refreshed, sauntered up to 65 York Street, and ascended to the 10th floor, to the offices of *Australia's Amateur Hour*. I'd already bluffed my way into a music publishers and a recording company today, so why not a radio show as well?

I went in and confidently requested to see Mr. Terry Dear, the show's star compere. Amazingly, my request was granted. I'm beginning to get the hang of this, I smiled to myself, as I was shown to his office. I'd already worked out precisely what I was going to say - I was going to tell him that I would be recording soon for EMI. I was convinced it would swing things my way and he'd have to assign me for the show. I knocked on the door and his familiar voice bade me enter.

Ten minutes later, I was walking out of that same door, with my feet hardly touching the ground. He'd swallowed my story, asked me to sing for him there and then and, liking what he heard, had offered me a date. I skipped down the corridor, silent yahoo's echoing triumphantly in my head. I paused in reception, grinned broadly at the girl on the desk and asked importantly if I might use the phone to call Mr. Wills at EMI. He wasn't in his office, so I left a message with his secretary:

I Remember Me

"Please tell Mr. Wills I shall be appearing on *Amateur Hour* on November 6th," I said, and put the phone down with a huge sigh of relief.

I sank deep into my seat on the train, surrounded by an aura of smug satisfaction. On the way home I mused over how I, a fourteen-year old schoolboy, had, all in one day, forced myself upon the top executives of Southern Music, EMI Records and *Amateur Hour*. What's more, I had successfully played one off against the other to win for myself a booking on a network radio show and the likely promise of a top recording contract - plus, of course, a new song, which was what I'd set out for in the first place.

Suddenly, I sat bolt upright in my seat. A terrible thought had just hit me. What on earth was I going to tell my parents when I got home?

-8-
WE'RE ON THE AIR

What on earth was I going to say? I hated the thought of spoiling my great victory by shrouding it beneath lies and alibis. But what else could I do? Tell my dad exactly what happened? Tell him that now I had an assured future in music, school was irrelevant and I intended to leave once and for all? A vision of my father, apoplectic in anger, floated up before me and I shuddered.

On the other hand, maybe I could walk in as if nothing had happened? This was the easy option and was tempting, but how could I hide my excitement, my late arrival home and, more to the point, explain how I came by a contract to appear on *Australia's Amateur Hour*?

As I made my way from the station and up our road, I finally settled on what I would do. I decided it was best to stick to the truth - but only as much truth as I reckoned to be safe. I pushed open the door, bubbling with excitement. Firstly, I told Mum all about being accepted for *Australia's Amateur Hour* then sheepishly confessed I'd skipped sports afternoon at school in order to try for the show. Since I had not missed any lessons, I got away with it, which was just as well since I'd need Mum's signature on my contract. I omitted to tell her the rest of the story, reckoning that if EMI Records did want to record me, it would just seem to be as a natural result of my appearance.

However, my mind still churned with the momentous events of the day and I needed to pour out the entire story to a sympathetic ear. I went to find Lorraine.

I had first sighted Lorraine one mellow evening some months before, when I had been strolling through the centre of the village of Beecroft engaged in the infinitely absorbing pastime of watching the girls go by. Dressed in her eye-catching, short green gym-slip, she was just emerging from her keep fit class, her pretty schoolgirl complexion enhanced by the healthy glow of recent exertion and a rash of freckles. She cut short my inane chat-up line with a slice of garlic sausage. If she proffered it as a defence against amorous advances, then it worked. I chewed while she chatted and I found myself totally at ease with her.

We became friends - a carefree, uncomplicated companionship, unfettered by the strings of emotion. We simply enjoyed one another's company, my freewheeling spirit finding an affinity with her ingenuous love of life. There was nothing half-hearted about Lorraine. She would immerse herself totally in everything she did. When we went to the movies, she would sit there wide-eyed, utterly engrossed in the film, feeding her open mouth with a continuous supply of Jaffa sweets. Then would come the inevitable moment when the box would slide off her lap, the sweets would go rattling all over the hardwood floor and up would go the cry "Lorraine's in!".

So it was Lorraine I turned to as the haven where I could safely let free my wild excitement. She shared my anxieties and bolstered my confidence in those interminable days while I waited for *Amateur Hour* to materialise.

Amateur Hour was Australia's premier radio showcase for new talent. It was broadcast nation-wide every Thursday via the Macquarie network, and had a large listening public who were asked to vote for their favourite performer. To win was a tremendous boost for an artist's career, and there was such stiff competition to gain a place on the show that, until forced into it, I hadn't given much thought as to whether or not I was ready. However, now I had my place on the show, the imperative was for me to be the winner. Would Ron Wills want to sign up a singer who was only second best? Would bookings for stage and radio come flooding in to the performer whom nobody wanted to listen to? I convinced myself that anywhere short of first place would be utter disaster.

Lorraine volunteered to act as my campaign manager. She prowled the entire neighbourhood, pleading, cajoling, coaxing and bribing a vote for me out of everyone she could possibly catch in her clutches. Meanwhile, I occupied every spare moment practising the song I had chosen to sing - the Wilf Carter song *There's A Love Knot In My Lariat*.

November 6th finally arrived and I spent the entire morning fretting in an agony of expectation. Mum packed my special black western outfit complete with hat and everybody gathered to give me a great send-off.

The 2GB auditorium was bristling with budding hopefuls like myself, nervously shuffling their feet. I looked my competition over and although we seemed poor, pitiful aspirants, one of these ten acts would nevertheless emerge victorious. I was determined it would be me. Why else had Destiny brought me here?

Unfortunately, I'd drawn the position of being third act on - before the studio audience really had time to warm up. Confidence calmed my nerves, and when my turn came to step before the microphone, I was cool, calm and collected as I took up my guitar. I gave my all to my song - it never sounded better to my ears, and my yodel was as clear as a bell. Enthusiastic applause confirmed my opinion, and the phone-in votes quickly mounted in my favour, surpassing the thousand-mark before the show was even half way through. Closing in on my heels, however, was a young operatic singer who sang *Most Amusing* - and she was good, very good in fact. Yet at the end of the programme, I led the field.

The show was over, but the ordeal was just starting. The winner wouldn't be known until all the postal votes were counted, and the final results would be announced on next week's broadcast. Lorraine redoubled her efforts, pleading with friends, neighbours, schoolmates and even total strangers to write in with a vote for me. "How many?" I kept asking. "Hundreds!" she would confidently reply. The seven days of waiting were impossibly tense and by the time we'd gathered round the radio at home to hear the results, my nerves were stretched as tight as the strings of my guitar. Then, there it was at last - my name was being announced with the number of votes I'd won. Cheers broke out, threatening to erupt through the roof.

Performing on Radio 2GB's *Amateur Hour* in 1952, aged 14.

I Remember Me

"How many? How many did they say?" I demanded, above the din.

The voice on the radio babbled on, and suddenly the cheers around me were stifled. Loud and clear, over the airwaves, another name was announced. I had been beaten into second place by the opera singer with that *Most Amusing* song. I was not amused - I was devastated.

Everyone crowded around to congratulate me, saying what a wonderful achievement it was to have come second, how proud I must be that I'd got so many votes. But I was inconsolable. As far as I was concerned, I'd blown my chances. All the build-up and tension, all the preparation, all those whoppers I'd told on that day in Sydney, and all for what?

Nothing.

I raced out of the room and out of the house. Sitting alone out on the patio, I broke down and sobbed uncontrollably, tears of self-pity mixed with frustration and despair. Then, as the sobbing subsided, into my mind came one of my father's wise sayings:

"The glory is not in never falling - but in the rising each time you fall."

Of course, it wasn't the end of the race; I'd just tripped over a hurdle. Nobody can expect Destiny to prepare a clear course - I had to make most of the running myself. I determined to pick myself up, dust myself off, and re-enter the fray.

My resolve started with Tim McNamara. I'd been playing his shows for the best part of a year now, and in all that time, my payment had remained at the measly sum of one pound and one shilling. I would soon be fifteen and, therefore, in my estimation, was no longer just a pushover kid. I confronted Tim after a show at the Kensington Town Hall. His reaction? Suffice to say, I got the sack.

It didn't matter, though, for Tim's ex-wife Daphne stepped into the breach. She'd heard about my heated exchange with Tim and hired me on the spot at double the fee. Never mind *Amateur Hour*, my fame was on the rise, and the proof of it came when popular weekly magazine *Pix*, in a feature on the Hillbilly boom, printed a full-page photograph of myself.

With this kind of success on my side, I was loath to return to school. At fifteen, I could quite legitimately leave, and since a showbiz career was what I wanted, I didn't see the need for any further education - but I knew my parents wouldn't see it that way. So I started playing hooky, leaving the house each morning as if heading for school, then sloping off to while away the day in pursuit of my dreams.

But I hadn't counted on my school report. The damning evidence now lay exposed in the powerful hands of my father, and my heart sank to my shoes as I dragged open the door and slunk into the room to face him. I can see him now, indignant, stern-faced, and red with rage as he tossed the envelope on the floor in disgust.

"This report is absolutely abysmal. Don't you realise how important your schooling is? You've been backsliding, and worse still, you've been devious and underhanded. Did you think you could pull the wool over our eyes?"

I had it coming, I knew. Standing there before him, quaking to my very roots, I realised I should have been up-front with him and told him earlier of my frustrations over school. By being sneaky, I'd taken the coward's way out. However, I didn't expect the tirade that followed.

"It's all because of these silly Hillbilly shows you've been doing isn't it? They're filling your head with highfalutin' ideas, aren't they? Well let me tell you my lad, if you don't go back and finish your schooling, I'll have to ground you."

So shocked was I by this that my voice wouldn't come out. I just stared, open-mouthed.

"Huh. To think that a son of mine should ever even consider a full time professional career in the precarious entertainment business."

Up until this moment, I wasn't even aware Dad knew what I was doing. Oh, I knew my taste in records annoyed him intensely, and he was always telling me to turn down the volume, or to stop singing and help him in the garden, but to know about my ambition and object to it before I'd even started? I had to show him I was serious.

"But Dad, I'm already working..."

"Working – ha! Is that what you call it? It's not a proper job. It's a fickle business, full of lay-abouts, ne'er-do-wells and confidence tricksters."

I viewed his argument as totally illogical and unreasonable.

"It's not true! They're really nice people..."

"I won't hear another word! I had something better in mind for my sons, something respectable and dependable like... like engineering. To qualify for that or, indeed, any decent profession, you need your schooling. So it's back to school tomorrow my lad or, I repeat, you'll be grounded."

I had no alternative. He did indeed have the power to ground me, and what's more, legally I needed one of my parents to sign my contracts

I Remember Me

until I was twenty-one, and there was no way Mum would do that without Dad's approval.

He reminded me I had less than one year left before the Intermediate Certificate exam. "And," he said, "if you put your mind to it, you can still pass."

With head hung low, I gave my solemn promise to do as he wished. The whole room was emotionally charged, and I left it feeling shattered. I couldn't understand why he wouldn't listen to me, wouldn't even give me chance to prove myself. It seemed so out of character. What I wasn't aware of at the time and only learned much later, was that some years earlier, back in England, he'd lost much of his hard-earned savings by staging a concert recital for his opera-trained brother Jeff. Based on that experience, Dad was determined to defend himself and his progeny against the pain of any other such disaster.

That was all very well - but in his well-meaning protectiveness, he'd left me totally wretched. Just as the doors were starting to open for a promising future, they had been well and truly slammed shut in my face. I rushed out of the house and into the streets, in headlong flight to somewhere, anywhere, where I could hide my red face and the insurgent tears.

When I returned from licking my wounds, I found Mum standing in the hall with a strange expression on her face.

"Sit down, Frank," she commanded, and the unaccustomed severity in her voice made me do as she bid without question. Here we go, I thought, now it's Mum's turn to have a go at me, and I don't blame her.

"You've just had a phone call."

She paused, and I was alarmed. Oh dear, now what's gone wrong?

"It was from a Mr. Ron Wills of EMI." Suddenly her face was all smiles. "He's asked you to attend an audition for a recording contract!"

For a split second, I was speechless, unable to take it all in. Then I jumped up, grabbed Mum in my arms and danced her up and down the hall, whooping in glee at the top of my voice.

"When? Oh, when?" I demanded.

She opened the diary to show me. There, under the date Tuesday May 10th 1953, she had scribbled: Audition 4.45pm.

However, there was an obstacle still to overcome: Dad. Without his permission, the engagement couldn't take place at all.

Mum tried to reassure me. "You've promised to return to school, haven't you?"

I nodded.

"Well then, if you can show him you're serious in your intentions and you're willing to work hard towards your goal, he won't stand in your way. But you must be honest, because it's dishonesty and deviousness he will not tolerate."

I was beginning to understand just how irresponsible my behaviour must have appeared in my parents' eyes.

"Will you help me?" I pleaded.

"We'll speak to him together," she said.

Much to my relief, the EMI audition was sanctioned, and Mum journeyed with me and my guitar to EMI in Homebush on May 10th, after school. I was so excited, I almost wet my pants. I felt faintly ridiculous, standing there in my school uniform, yet I managed to remain cool, calm and businesslike while Mr Wills explained he wanted to make two records in the same session. I sang a range of songs, and we settled on the one I performed on *Australia's Amateur Hour* backed by the one I had previously sung for him in his office, plus Hank Snow's *Broken Dreams* coupled with my own composition *Valley of Love*.

When finally all was signed and sealed, Mum and I left the office. Once out in the street, we cheered - and we couldn't stop grinning at each other all the way home.

By today's standards, the recording session was a primitive affair, but to my inexperienced young eyes, it was intimidating. I was directed to my position by the microphone - a huge, bulky affair that hung menacingly in front of my face and blotted out my view. People were swarming around me, competently setting up this and tweaking with that, but suddenly they all disappeared, leaving me and my voice to brave the ordeal on our own. I stood there watching for the red light, my only contact with the outside world, and when it came on, I began. It was like singing in a potato sack - the walls were hung with rough hessian that seemed to absorb my voice and refuse to sound it back to me.

It sure was a nerve-racking experience, as I had only two chances to get it right. Since there were no tape recorders in those days, the recording was made direct to disc, which means what it says - my voice and guitar were recorded directly onto a wax disc impression. There was no such thing as stereo, or even hi-fi, because they hadn't yet been invented. So, in order to enhance the effect of my yodel, they applied an echo to it. They told me this was achieved by the use of an echo chamber and I was impressed, until I learned this meant passing my falsetto through the toilet, keeping fingers crossed that no-one was caught short during the time of recording.

I Remember Me

All right, so it was all a bit crude, but what the heck. For all its shortcomings, the results were eminently presentable, and I, for one, was delighted with the outcome of the day's work.

♪♫♪♫♪

Now I had regular professional gigs and a record release in the offing, the next step had to be radio. In the time before television, Australian radio was the lifeblood of our industry. Over the nation, there were 108 commercial and 54 national broadcasting stations. Sydney itself had six independent commercial radio stations broadcasting from the inner city, and two, government funded, national ABC stations. Most of the shows were live broadcasts, and helped forge the Australian identity by promoting home-grown product.

Fully professional radio shows were, as yet, beyond my sphere, or so I thought. So I was totally surprised by the invitation, sent by 2GB, to attend an audition for their new weekly country-style series *Bonnington's Bunkhouse Show*. No mere small station offering, this was to be a lavish production, with a format of comedy sketches and music that put me in mind of the BBC radio shows I used to listen to in England, like ITMA and *Much Binding In The Marsh*. It was to be recorded at the 2GB playhouse in front of a live audience, and replayed Australia-wide via the Macquarie network. Talk about a shot at the big time.

I went along, fingers crossed and full of hope. However, I felt a greenhorn among all the well-known performers, and didn't expect to be chosen - and I wasn't. I was by-passed in favour of country singer, Reg Lindsay, who already had a record out on the new Rodeo label.

Nevertheless, opportunity still kept knocking - or rather, ringing - for a call came from the Catholic station, Radio 2SM, with a booking to appear live, each Saturday night, on a half-hour Country & Western show called *On The Trail*. This was to be a new programme to replace the *Tim McNamara Show*, and I was chosen to appear as a regular alongside Reg Lindsay, Nev Nichols, Kevin King, Nola Hurst and my new-found friend, Jimmy Little with his trio. Gentleman Jim is an Aborigine, and must rank as not only the first, but also the best recording country singing star of his race, and we hit it off right from the start.

This show didn't have quite the prestige of *Bonnington's Bunkhouse*, since Radio 2SM broadcast only to the greater Sydney area, but all the same, I was thrilled to be so frequently on the air. Within two weeks, I was on the air even more, when 2SM booked me to appear on a regular basis on a further two of their shows, *Can we help you?* with Tommy Jay and *Pappy's Show*.

The exposure I was receiving soon brought me to the notice of the major network station 2UE, where they offered me a regular role in their new weekly programme *Vincent's Youth Parade* hosted by their top deejay, Howard Craven. Then, hot on the heels of my first appearance, came yet another contract with them, for my very own weekly half-hour show. Called *Sundown Singsong*, it was recorded at their ultra-modern studios, and syndicated all over Australia. I dished up a wide variety of music, but always included a recipe of songs with a strong Aussie flavour. In addition to my guitar, Frank Scott played piano and Des Tanner provided colourful accompaniment on the organ, while actor and film star Charles Tingwell, known as Bud, did the narration.

I distinctly remember my first meeting with Charles, because he insisted he couldn't work with me unless I was a member of Actor's Equity. I stared at him, for as a fifteen-year-old lad still at school, such matters as union membership were way beyond my reckoning. But my admiration for his professional standing, and the honour I felt at having him on my show, made me pay my dues the very next day. Soon after completing the series, Charles upped and left for England, where he was to become even more successful, while I would be stuck paying out three pounds, sixteen shillings a year membership for ever more.

By the end of August 1953, I was appearing regularly on four radio shows a week, plus my stage shows at weekends. I had to put aside time at home to research and rehearse material for of all these shows, especially my own. Added to that were 5 days a week at school plus homework. In order to appease my father, I was under pressure, not just to attend school, but to try my hardest to pass the exams. Mum was behind me, regulating the work I took on, and helping me through it, while Dad seemed to fade into the background - and I kept out of his way.

Then, to cap it all off, on September 2nd 1953, came the offer of an ongoing contract to appear on *Bonnington's Bunkhouse* - an indication of just how far I had come in four short months. There really wasn't time in my overcrowded week to add yet another show, but this was an opportunity not to be missed, so somehow or other, I simply had to cram it in. Replacing Reg Lindsay made me feel bad, especially since we were still appearing together at 2SM's *On The Trail*, but Fate in her wisdom had determined this was my time.

And what a wonderful time it was. The show had a glittering cast and afforded me the chance to work with some of the greatest names in

I Remember Me

Australian radio: variety veteran George Foster; the deep, authoritative voice of actor Leonard Theale; the ever-popular comedian Keith Walshe; Country singing duo The McKean Sisters; producer-actor Noel Judd; the fine baritone voice of Neil Williams; the legendary London born actress Queenie Ashton; the Bunkhouse Band directed by Gus Mersey; and, on occasions which I looked forward to with enormous anticipation, the heavenly Lily Connors - she who I'd placed high on a pedestal when I was a mere novice in Eden Park. Her mother still came with her in the role of guardian and minder, but now I was working with her, I could legitimately approach her as a fellow artiste. That, however, was as near as my shyness – and her mother - would allow.

Naturally, I took the opportunity to promote my upcoming debut record, which, strangely enough, was released on November 5th 1953, precisely one year after my appearance on *Amateur Hour*. Strange too, it was as if I had had a premonition when I fabricated my story to music publisher Allan Crawford, because it did indeed appear on the distinctive green and red label of Regal Zonophone.

So proud was I, holding my first record gingerly in my hands, I couldn't stop reading my name on the label, again and again - and all the small print too, right down to its serial number, G25371. The aroma of its newness was the sweet smell of success, and I played it over and over again. When it started to show signs of scratching, I went out to buy a new one. It felt peculiar having to ask for a record bearing my own name, especially when the storekeeper, not knowing who I was, told me it was fortunate he still had one in stock, since it was proving to be very popular.

Meanwhile, at school things were changing for me. My friends felt they themselves were part of all that was happening, and even the teachers showed their pride in me by playing my record to the class. From being just a nobody, I was suddenly flavour of the moment. Girls who'd not even noticed I existed before, now buzzed around me like the proverbial bees round a honey pot. Why even Jeanette started to find me attractive now I was obviously going places.

My whole family was excited too; even my father couldn't disguise his grin of pleasure, as he offered a favourable critique on my record. I was a little surprised and enormously relieved. He told me that maybe, just maybe, he might reconsider his attitude to my singing, but it all depended on the effort I applied to my schoolwork.

So there was nothing for it but to knuckle down to my studying. True to my promise, and in spite of all my outside activities, I had diligently applied myself to my school work, surprising myself with my capabilities

We're On The Air

once the incentive was there to aid my concentration. Trying my damnedest to do my best, while bracing myself for the worst, I sat the dreaded exams. I was determined to pass, and pass I did. In my father's eyes, the gaining of my Intermediate Certificate was probably one of my greatest achievements - perhaps of even greater significance to him than any future awards and accolades, because I'd achieved it entirely through my own efforts. Even though I've never had reason to present those hard-earned credentials, it pleased me to know that my parents were proud of me.

Most importantly though, by passing the exams, I also gained my father's reluctant blessing for my chosen career. So, on December 15th 1953, fifteen days after my sixteenth birthday, I left school as fast as my legs could carry me.

-9-

URBAN COWBOY

"Are you a real cowboy?" they demanded, as I tried to clamber out of the car.

Pat must have spread the news that a famous cowboy was coming to pay them a visit, because as soon as we drove up, all the local young-uns gathered around in an excited crowd.

"Yeah," I drawled, casually tipping back the brim of my Stetson. I could hardly say "no", could I, with a gaggle of young admirers trapping me against the door? They might just be whippersnappers but I needed to maintain some credibility here.

"What can you do then?"

Just to say I sang cowboy songs seemed a bit feeble. "Oh, I can twirl a lariat," I bragged, "and I crack a stock-whip." After all, it was somewhat true, since I'd been taught a few tricks by Malcolm Mason who did a speciality act on the McNamara shows.

With that, they dragged me across to a nearby paddock and before I had time to draw breath, they shoved the implements into my hands. I ran through my repertoire for them. They were surprisingly quiet throughout this performance, but I put it down to sheer amazement at my prowess. In fact, I quite impressed myself by my abilities so when I turned to face them, I was feeling pretty puffed up with pride.

Children, especially, are very forthcoming with their reactions - and I got them all: jeers, sneers, hisses, hoots, howls, the lot. Of course, I hadn't figured out that, to these kids, having been brought up in the country, such skills were almost second nature. They offered to show me how it should be done and I have to admit I was outclassed. With their laughter burning rings round my embarrassment, I slunk off across the paddock, back to Pat.

Pat wasn't much help. He stood there, arms folded, smiling broadly at my discomfort. Pat Shaw, who looked a little like a young Audie Murphy, was a fellow who worked at Beecroft railway station and declared he was a fan of mine. He came from up-country near Kempsey and was always insisting I go up there and meet his family. With school finished, I finally found some spare time and Mum agreed I was in need of a holiday.

Urban Cowboy

The 'urban cowboy' – a fully fledged professional entertainer.

I Remember Me

So here I was, out in the country, nursing a bruised ego. However, the warm welcome from Pat's family soon lifted my spirits and I settled down to relax in their company. It appeared the episode was forgotten, but I hadn't reckoned on the cunning or the scheming of those little snotty-nosed kids.

The Willawarrin Agriculture Show was the high spot of the year here and it was to take place during my stay. Pat and his family were going and asked me to join them. I loved the showground atmosphere, strolling around the attractions, candyfloss in hand, and thrilling to the main-ring rodeo events.

The highlight of the afternoon was the buckjumping and we stood at the ringside eagerly awaiting the spectacle of brawny stockmen attempting to ride Brahman bulls. I'd seen these mean animals earlier, barred up safely in their well-fortified enclosure. Not only were they built like a tank but also they had a large shoulder hump with loose rolling skin that made it nigh impossible for a rider to maintain his hold.

The barricade was removed. Out gushed the first brute like a torrent from its bed, snorting in passion as it bucked around the ring. Its rider, a broad, muscle-bound giant of a man, didn't last long before he was floundering in the dust. With exceptional nimbleness for such a large man, he regained his feet and rushed to the barrier for safety just before the brute bore down upon him.

"Phew," I gasped at Pat; "You need to be some kind of a gallah to want to do that!" and I turned to await the next contestant with keen anticipation.

As well I might. His name was being announced over the loudspeaker and it was a very familiar name - mine! I thought I was hearing things, but no, there it was again and Pat was nudging me in the ribs. I looked at him dumbfounded. With blood thumping in my ears and my heart pounding madly, I set off for the competitors' enclosure, trying to visualise myself on board one of those monster man-eaters.

Needless to say I chickened out, confessing I was only a singing cowboy. I was asked to prove it by performing a song and thankfully the crowd forgave me. It was, of course, those young scrub cockies who'd put me up for it. I stamped off to stalk them out, vengeance surging through my veins, but fortunately for them, they'd already made themselves scarce.

We managed to laugh it off later that evening in the pub as I sat with Pat and his friends. It was while we were chatting over a schooner of lager the idea came up that I should put on an impromptu show at the local hall, and it seemed an ideal opportunity for me to regain some semblance of credibility in the neighbourhood. However, it was already Friday and I was to return home on Sunday.

"When can we do it?" I asked.

"Tomorrow night of course," was the reply. Obviously, not being professionals like me, they couldn't see the impossibility of putting together a show and gathering an audience in such a short space of time - and I told them so.

"Aw, don't worry mate, she'll be right."

And she was. I was amazed. Evidently, the town's efficient 'bush telegraph' had soon passed the news around and the hall was packed with country folk from every station within a hundred miles. A squeeze-box player was kidnapped from the local pub to provide the music for dancing, after which I did my turn. I was greeted with an uproar of applause and was feted for the rest of the evening on steaks and beer. I'd heard of overnight stardom, but this was incredible.

I left the following day with my dignity intact and my fame far-flung over the entire area. Cowering in the background, as I took my leave, was that band of sneaky kids. With great generosity of soul, I threw them a cheery wave as the car took off along the road, covering them in a cloud of red dust.

♪ ♫ ♪ ♫ ♪

I returned home to find Mum had been busy on my behalf. Proudly she displayed an engagement book bursting with dates. Because of my record release and radio exposure, theatrical agents were taking notice and offers had been coming in from all over. Freed from the constraints of school, I was at last able to take advantage of these and Mum soon had a full diary of bookings for me.

Amongst the dates, there was a preponderance of the Hillbilly shows such as I'd been working on Friday and Saturday nights these last two years for Tim then Daphne McNamara, and now Ted Quigg had also taken me on as a headliner for his shows. I enjoyed making the rounds of concert halls in those early Country and Western music shows, and I learned such a lot working with people I admired, like the ever-popular Slim Dusty and my all-time favourite whispering yodeller friend George Payne. I also absorbed everything I could from watching top comedians like Buster Noble, Slim DeGray, Al Thomas and Freddie Meredith and the speciality act of Malcolm Mason – he who had shown me how to spin

I Remember Me

a lariat and crack a stockwhip, much to my near undoing. Even so, I was justifiably proud of those skills back then, though today they are relegated to being just the twirling of a microphone cord.

By this time, my fame and fan following had projected me to top billing on these Country shows, but nevertheless I was still just part of a larger company. However, also in my diary were beginning to appear bookings for solo performances at private parties, clubs, pubs and beer-gardens. This was a new departure for me. I knew Mum was concerned about how I would cope on my own in some of the less reputable places, but she'd accepted the dates knowing I needed the wider experience.

She was right to be anxious. Australian pubs and clubs of the fifties could be rough and ready places, where stage entertainment took second place to the drink. I was well under the legal age, too, at sixteen, but since I looked mature for my age, nobody asked - and I certainly didn't tell them.

I found the undisciplined rabble tough to contend with after being accustomed to the more discerning theatre audiences. Before I could get anywhere, I had first to win them away from the bar. Then once I'd got 'em, I had to hold 'em and that was even more difficult. To begin with, I tried to give them my own style of music, but soon found it was a sure way to lose them back to the booze. These crowds were vociferous in demanding what they wanted - and it was not Country and Western. No, their only knowledge of music was the Top Ten and they called for the latest American hits. So even though I felt it somewhat cramped my style, I had no choice but to give them what they demanded. Nevertheless, I rendered the songs in my own manner and, on the whole, they were satisfied with that.

If I wasn't out twanging my guitar, I'd be doing the rounds of the radio stations. All those shows I'd started on while at school were still running and by the time I reached my seventeenth birthday, I reckon I could count myself as one of the most experienced radio performers in Sydney. In fact, my frequent visits to 2SM prompted their receptionist to suggest I bring my bed in.

It was on one of my visits to 2SM that I found myself collared by their top deejay, Tony Withers. He manoeuvred me into a quiet corner and proceeded to pour his undoubted charm in my direction. What had I done to deserve this attention all of a sudden? There could only be one reason - he wanted something from me.

"Hmm, Frank," he said, clearing his throat of some imaginary obstruction, "you wouldn't do me a favour, would you?"

"Ye-ess?" I said slowly, on the defensive.

"You know Radio 2UE?"

Of course I did - I was still appearing every week in the *Youth Parade* show.

"Ye-ess."

"Well, they manage to get all the latest American hit records to play, don't they? So they must have them in their library. You couldn't use your influence to 'borrow' some for a few hours, could you? I... I'd like to conduct a little experiment." And he proceeded to explain.

Some experiment.

I admired Tony as a deejay and what's more, his daring plan appealed to my wicked sense of mischief, so I agreed. Now it was my turn to use my charm, this time on the record librarian of 2UE. He accepted my story that I needed to borrow the records in order to update my material for *Youth Parade* so, somewhat reluctantly, he lent them to me.

"Bring them back tomorrow, or there'll be hell to pay," he shouted at my retreating rear.

With this threat hovering over me, I crept furtively into the studios of 2SM with my booty. Tony grabbed the discs, rushed into his little broadcasting booth and barricaded himself firmly inside. I watched through the window where, following the Angelus, I saw the red light flashing 'On Air'. Then, instead of the quiet dinner music he was supposed to play, he let rip with the American Hit Parade.

While the airwaves reverberated to the furious beat of the latest hit, the corridors of 2SM echoed to the beat of furious feet pounding beneath the station manager on his mad dash towards Tony's studio. His raging attempts to block the programme were to no avail; Tony was firmly ensconced and nothing less than an earthquake would move him until he'd finished. Short of taking the station off the air, there was not a lot the manager could do.

Naturally, when he finally did emerge after this unscheduled programme, Tony got the sack - but this action only proved a further embarrassment for the station, for such was the enormously favourable public response to the programme, he had to be reinstated at a much higher fee. The management was unaware of my involvement in this madcap scheme so I hope the intervening years have honed their sense of humour.

John Brennan was another of the 2SM 'Good Guy' disc jockeys for whom I had a high regard. He suffered a bad stutter, yet managed to conquer it totally when on the air. In fact there was no-one to touch him

I Remember Me

for clarity of diction and I aspired to be like him when broadcasting. We, too, were involved in an experimental scheme, only this time it was with official blessing. Together we compiled the first Country Music Hit Parade in Sydney, which was broadcast once a week and encompassed the hits of artists such as Jim Reeves, Marty Robbins, Don Gibson, Tennessee Ernie Ford and many others. We also featured the best Australian country recordings and, naturally, I included myself - which did my record sales no harm at all.

By the end of 1954, I'd had three record releases. The second was *Broken Dreams* and *Valley of Love*, while the third was the song my Dad used to sing to us, *Abdul Abulbul Amir*, coupled with the song I had written in dedication to my mum, *A Mothers Faith*. There were two more in the can ready to start off 1955, and yet another for release in the June called *Yodelling Mad*.

I was fortunate, earning a decent living from radio, recording and my live shows but, creatively, I knew I was never going to be satisfied with life just as it was. As I travelled with my guitar from the poky dressing room of a dusty little theatre to the gritty boards of the next rowdy pub, I was visualising the targets where this Archer would eventually aim his arrows. I was aiming high. Five major targets I set myself - the prestigious London Palladium, The Olympia in Paris, Las Vegas, that Mecca for Country music, Nashville's Grand Ole Opry, and, my first objective, Sydney's Tivoli Theatre. The Tivoli was never to be. Could it have been I wasn't considered good enough or was it that they were looking more towards booking overseas acts? I will never know. Be that as it may, to achieve these ambitions, I knew I was going to have to develop way beyond the cosy confines of my Country Music shows.

Indeed, the innocent years were coming to an end. The advent of 1955 brought with it the taste of change in the air. My beloved Grandpa Peppa was now beginning to slow down - after all he was now into his mid eighties. So Mum and Dad decided Grandpa and Grandma would be better off in a new house closer to the city, as their old home in Arcadia was becoming just too much hard work for the pair of them. The garden was very big and Grandpa insisted on carrying buckets of water up from the creek for the flower beds.

It was the month of May when the time came for their move to Epping. Being nearer to us at Beecroft would make it a lot easier to keep an eye on both him and Grandma in the winter of their lives. In order that he would not over-exert himself, my brothers and I cleared the garden of soil and left the small back yard as bed rock - only to find that within a few days of moving in, Peppa had reversed our chore by wheelbarrowing all the soil back up and had already planted rows of little seedlings.

"If I cannot enjoy watching young things grow, life is not worth the effort," he stated firmly.

However, very shortly afterwards he took to his bed with pneumonia. I shall never forget that moment when my father came to me, saying I might now go in to pay my last respects. I remember sitting ever so quietly and respectfully at his bedside, conscious of the tick tock of the family heirloom as it gently broke the silence by marking down his last moments of time. I desperately wanted him to know my love for him, so I took hold of his hand. I felt him move his fingers slightly in acknowledgement of me and although his lips hardly moved, I'll swear he whispered, oh so softly yet calmly,

"Don't hold me back, this is beautiful."

Then he was quiet, bathed in the golden glow of the sunset. I had to let go of the hand of my eighty-seven year old hero as, on the evening of the sixth of June 1955, he left on his last travelling show, slipping away to wherever his dream of heaven was to lead him. His going, and that of his devoted wife who followed him soon afterwards, marked the end of an era.

It was not just for me, but for the whole world that change was on its way. The age of Rock 'n Roll was about to dawn.

-10-

SINGING THE KHAKI BLUES

Rock 'n Roll burst upon us like an atom bomb and in its wake came the rebellious teenage cults of bodgies and widgies, surfies and rockers and motorbike gangs. Every spare moment was spent on Bondi beach, soaking up the sun and riding the surf. It was an outdoor, carefree life of sand and sea, pies and prawns, beer and barbies and bikini-clad suntanned sheilas.

These were exciting, magical times and I rushed in to be a part of it all. I donned the obligatory peak cap and sunglasses and swanked around on my Army BSA motorcycle, making believe I was Marlon Brando as the Wild One, leading my gang from the seat of a Harley Davidson, or James Dean as a rebel without a cause with my arms around my favourite film star, Natalie Wood.

In reality though, my arms were around my new girl, Gabrielle. She was as cute as a button and every bit as pretty as any star of the silver screen - brunette and petite with a warm shy smile and a mischievous twinkle in her eyes.

How well I remember our first date. I was keen to make a good impression and, even though I say so myself, I cut quite a dash in my leathers. Astride my motorbike, I rounded the corner of her road, the excitement bubbling up inside me. She appeared on the doorstep, a vision of loveliness in her pretty white party dress with its full skirt and layers of fluffy petticoats. A shadow passed over her face at the sight of my battered old BSA, but she disguised it with a smile as she stepped gingerly towards me and clambered onto the pillion seat, enveloping us both in a cloud of tulle. It was at this moment I realised this relished old relic really had to go.

Fate apparently thought so too, for some time later, when I was riding solo, she played her hand, causing me to smash into a brick wall. Although my motorbike was a write-off, I wasn't injured save for my bruised pride and a gravel rash on my bum.

I set about saving up for a deposit on a car and, just in time for Christmas, I was able to purchase a steel-grey 1936 model Hudson Straight Eight that cost me £160 on the never-never. My progression from banger motorbike to this awesome American automobile might well have been a leap from the sublime to the ridiculous, but there was no denying my dates with Gabrielle were enhanced by the luxury of its roomy interior. Not only did it allow Gabrielle sufficient space to spread her ball gown, it could almost double for the ballroom itself.

My first true love, Gabrielle.
Her pretty white party dress enveloped us both in a cloud of tulle when she clambered onto the pillion seat of my motorbike on our first date.

I Remember Me

Fortunately, the acquisition of my limousine gave me freedom to expand the orbit of my work sphere, too, which was just as well, since the dynamism of the new music was threatening to undermine the very fabric of my career. Hillbilly had given way to Rock-a-billy, Country and Western had yielded to the jive. The live Hillbilly shows that had been my bread and butter were gradually disappearing, as were those once popular Country radio series that had brought me to public notice. One by one they were being taken off the air - my own *Sundown Singsong, The Bunkhouse Show* and even that stalwart, *Vincent's Youth Parade* all folded, overtaken by a growing demand for the Country-style rock of the wild Southern boys from Tennessee - Elvis Presley, Carl Perkins, Gene Vincent and Jerry Lee Lewis. It was obvious that to survive in show business, I would have to go with the flow.

I climbed in my car and travelled. I journeyed up the Blue Mountains to Katoomba, where I entered into a new role as a disc jockey on Radio 2KA 'The Voice Of The Mountains'. I decided to play records interspersed with live music provided by myself and guests who would just pop in with their guitars. The live section was entirely impromptu and the listeners' response proved they loved it.

I ventured further afield for my live shows, too, and although I knew it was vital to expand my audience like this, I lamented the way my work was depriving me of a normal everyday life and parting me from my family and my Gabrielle. There were compensations, especially when I appeared in the Wollongong area, for whenever I was there, I stayed with a couple who became very close mates of mine.

It was a shared love of Country music which had first brought me the acquaintance of Col Dennis and his wife Lorna. We met when I was playing at the Illawarra Leagues Club and Lorna, who was working there, took pity on my loneliness and invited me back to their house between shows. It was there we discovered that between us we must have had the biggest collection of Hank Snow records in Australia.

Col was a stock car enthusiast and his passion for the crash and bash game soon rubbed off on me. When we were young, Dad had taken my brothers and me to see many motorcycle races and though mechanical wizardry was way beyond me, I inherited from him the thrill of speedway. It only needed a whiff of racing fuel or the raw throbbing of a tuned engine to awaken the excitement and have me hooked.

Col lavished his love on a much coveted Cadillac, a monster of a car which was the scourge of the circuit. His profession was trucking and he was an expert driver. Many was the opponent who came to grief by hitting the rear of the Cadillac and flying over the top to his destruction. I was allowed occasionally to drive the car and put it through its paces and believe you me, this was some mean machine.

I was indeed proud when Col acknowledged me as his partner, displaying my name with his on the livery. "Another smash hit for Frank and Colin" would come over the loud speakers from Radio 2KY's circuit commentator, Reon Voight, as Col won yet another race.

I was proud to be partner to ace speedway driver, Col Dennis, and to have my name emblazoned across his mighty machines.

Col and Lorna were the exception, though, and in my travels I was often lonely. I deeply regretted not having enough time to spend with my Gabrielle. In her, I'd found my first taste of true love and I loved her dearly. The look of devotion that poured from her eyes gave me a warm, inner glow I carried with me everywhere I went. My nights off were far too precious to share her company with others and the old Hudson provided a haven of tranquillity, where we could indulge in the simple pleasures of togetherness, away from prying eyes.

Our favourite haunt was Kissing Point Road, where, parked in our regular spot, we had a magnificent view over the twinkling lights of Sydney. This place was inspirational, a place where we could share our

I Remember Me

dreams of the future. I opened up my heart to her about my wildest aspirations, the sort of heady ambitions I hardly dared admit to myself.

Hers, on the other hand, were the steady dreams of love and marriage and a future shared together. One day she asked me, in all seriousness, whether I'd be prepared to change my religion for her. It gave me a jolt. To me there was plenty of time before responsibilities needed to be faced, for after all, she was only 16 going on 17 while I was 18 and going on forever.

Perhaps I didn't take the question seriously enough, or maybe my dreams didn't include enough space for her? I don't know, for she never told me her reasons - she just upped and left me without a word. All I knew was, it was over and I would have to go it alone, but my heart wouldn't accept the fact. I dithered and drifted, unable to face up to a future without her. Not knowing why she had dumped me was slowly killing me. I needed a good shake up - and as I couldn't do it for myself, then Fate would have to step in and do it for me.

♪♫♪♫♪

Holsworthy Army Barracks had never seen such a daggy digger as the lovesick bombardier, number 2/755412 who, on Tuesday, April 24th 1956, reported for National Service training in the 13th Artillery Regiment. My heart wasn't into playing soldiers. I could only watch dejectedly as my fair hair fell to the floor, leaving me with a crew-cut that didn't suit me any more than it suited my blues to be wearing khaki. Nevertheless I resolved to see off this unwarranted interruption to my career as painlessly as possible by serving my time dutifully, without complaint.

My resolution was soon broken when, early in the peace, I was put on a charge for insulting the cooks. I've always been a good trencherman and the tucker was so abysmal I felt entirely justified – and, anyway, I did mop up the floor afterwards. I refused to be cowed into submission and as my protests continued so did my punishments: the inevitable 'Dixie bashing' (washing pans) or 'spud bashing' (peeling potatoes).

Fortunately for me, my brother John had been called up the previous year and he'd sussed out the lurks and perks to pass on to me. On his advice, I volunteered for the Intelligence Corps, where I would be spared the daily drudgery of the foot-slogger. In this division, my rank was elevated from bombardier to one star private, and consequently, I soon became known as 'Private I'.

Singing the Khaki Blues

It's well known that a soldier should never volunteer for anything, but John had also weighed up the advantages in offering up one's services for the much loathed latrine duties. This offered privileged access to a Jeep and trailer, not to mention carte blanche to pass freely back and forth through the main gates in order to gain access to the contamination grounds. Here I would leave the trailer, or 'muck truck' as it was known, to go joy riding in the Jeep, whilst keeping a watchful eye out for the Military Police.

If I landed this job on a Friday, I would lay in wait just outside the camp, Jeep at the ready, to offer my services as chauffeur to those on leave, undercutting the taxi fare to Ingleburn railway station and swelling my own coffers. I thought I displayed a definite flair for flaunting the rules but evidently I lacked the vigilance needed to make a total success of it, often getting caught AWOL.

One night when I'd been confined to barracks, I was particularly determined to keep a date with a pretty young lady. I drove my jalopy - my old Hudson now nicknamed Big Bertha - slowly towards the barrack gate. As I approached, I applied full choke and, with a cloud of black smoke, she backfired, coughed and ground to a halt. Making sure the guard saw me, I got out to push, puffing and blowing behind the bulk of Big Bertha.

The sentry challenged me, then asked "Got trouble with the car, mate?"

"Yeh," said I, innocently, "it just zonked out and the battery's gone flat. You couldn't give us a push, could you?"

"Hey lads!" he yelled in the direction of a group of straggling soldiers, "Come here a minute. We've got a problem."

I clambered hastily into the driving seat and the lads dutifully obliged by shoving Big Bertha and myself through the gates, where I continued down the hill. The incident was never reported – I wonder why?

Training was intensive and I felt as though I was being shoved through a sausage machine. I'd started as a bombardier, gone on to Intelligence as a private and finally ended up as a gunner. I protested at this last switch, pointing out that operations on the 45-pounder guns could injure my hearing, which was essential to my career in civilian life. Joyously, my complaint fell on sympathetic ears and I spent the last weeks in the more congenial role of staging shows for the Officers' Mess. At last I'd found something in this soldiering game in which I could excel, for I came away presented with a souvenir pewter beer mug bearing the insignia of the Australian Army Corps, for my efforts.

I Remember Me

Demobbed and determined to get myself as far from the Army's clutches as I possibly could, I took off to Queensland with my brother John and friends 'Mad-dog' Quadling and Jim Kirby. But the trip very nearly ended in disaster. It was all Big Bertha's fault. Having survived the Army intact, the old girl started to develop problems as soon as she encountered civilian life once more.

She was not firing on all eight cylinders when we set off, but nevertheless she kept going and so did we. However, somewhere, marked on the map as nowhere, miles from anywhere, she broke a spring. It was my big hero brother who saved the day. With great ingenuity, he cut down a sapling and used it as a replacement spring. We continued our journey, albeit a bit lopsided.

All went well until, on our return journey, the old car started to lose water. Now, this is very dangerous when you are out alone in the dry desolate country, hours from habitation, with nothing in the way of passing traffic. We stopped at every creek bed and filled with whatever liquid it offered. The stench of boiling tadpoles and algae was pungent to say the least but we managed to keep motoring.

At last, however, the inevitable happened and we came to a grinding halt, boiled dry with no water to be found anywhere. The only liquid to be had was in the few remaining bottles of beer we were carrying. Were we to save it for our own salvation, or gamble on giving it to Bertha in the hope she would take us to our rescue? It was put to a vote and the unanimous decision was to donate it to the car - but only after it had passed through our kidneys.

With our generous gift inside her, Big Bertha limped home, where we read her the last rites as she finally bit the dust.

♪♫♪♫♪

Whatever else the Army did for me, it did enable me regain a grasp on the things that mattered in my life and I came back home with my priorities sorted and my sense of purpose restored: nothing was more important than the precious love of my family - and being re-united with my faithful dog, Rover.

Oh, how we had missed each other while we had been apart. He was always my devoted friend and confidant, his trusting eyes overflowing with sympathy whenever the world seemed to let me down. He had the uncanny knack of being able to foretell exactly when I was coming home, even though my timetable was far from regular. Mum would always know

Singing the Khaki Blues

my train had arrived, for he would prick up his ears and set off running towards Beecroft station the moment I stepped onto the platform.

Whenever things went wrong, there was always a faithful friend to console me. Here I am with Drover.

Wonderful though it was to be home, there still remained the urgent necessity of getting my floundering career back on track. I was fortunate that stage shows and radio work soon began to flow in again and despite my enforced absence, my records were still selling well. It was enough to get me restarted, but I knew that to progress I would need to move with the times and that I would have a struggle ahead to find my role in the all-changing world of popular music.

Audiences who had been thrilled by their rock 'n roll heroes on film were coming to expect more from their own local performers, so artists were rushing in to copy the American hit makers. I wasn't ready to follow their trail and made a conscious decision then that I've steadfastly stuck to ever since: I determined to retain my individuality.

That doesn't mean to say I didn't change, I had to, but slowly and without letting the new-wave influences swamp my own style. I spent long hours investigating ways to update my presentation and I experimented in the recording studio, trying out some novel ideas with a song called *Gypsy Heart*, and my first rock 'n roll influenced track, my self-penned *Don't Do That*. It seemed to be appreciated, perhaps because instead of diving into the pool of conformity, I was now refreshingly different.

My hard work paid off when I had the good fortune to be chosen to perform at the Sydney Stadium for a week with Jimmie Rodgers, who was riding high on the success of his big hit *Kisses Sweeter Than Wine*.

Jimmie was the latest in a stream of star American attractions brought to the Stadium by Lee Gordon, the last of the big time Australian impresarios. If it weren't for Lee, Australia might well have remained a forgotten outpost in the wide world of entertainment. I'd been to see them all, from the magnetism of the legendary Buddy Holly, to the explosive energy of Eddie Cochrane and Gene Vincent, whose *Be-Bop-A-Lula* still ranks as one of my favourite records of the era. Then there was that superb showman, Sammy Davis Jr. and the captivating harmonies of the Platters, but it was undoubtedly Louis Armstrong who impressed me most, his genuine warmth generating such a loving response from his audience it left me spellbound.

And now it was my turn. The venue was certainly not built with concerts in mind. Its most distinctive feature, its revolving stage, only resulted in giving everyone an equally bad view, and the acoustics were dreadful. Nevertheless, because of its large capacity and ability to attract the world's superstars, it became the most important showcase in Sydney.

I was incredibly nervous, yet extremely proud because my dad had promised to attend my opening night. It was the first time he had come to one of my shows and it meant he had finally acknowledged my chosen career. However, he made one proviso - I must sing his favourite song *I Believe*, as he thought it suited my voice.

Now, I'd put a lot of time and deliberation into choosing my programme and definitely had not included this one. The idea scared me to death - to sing this slow ballad at a rock concert could be suicidal. Did I choose to ignore my father and risk alienating him just when he had offered to breach the rift between us, or did I choose to respect his wishes and invite possible ruination to befall the new blossoming of my career?

My father couldn't understand my predicament. Yet, so important was his approval that reluctantly, I agreed... and as the last note of the song echoed around the walls of the huge auditorium, the audience was so silent I could hear my heart pounding. There followed the longest moment of my life while I stared disaster in the face, trying hard to choke back my desperation. Then... to my disbelieving ears, wild applause broke out and I saw the smug look on Dad's face as, one by one, the entire audience sprang to their feet and he witnessed a standing ovation.

The show was compered by one of Australia's top deejays - Graham Webb. We'd known one another a long time, as our work on Radio 2SM brought us into frequent contact, and one night later in the week, while chatting to him in the overcrowded main dressing room, I happened to mention my car was in dock. Without hesitation, he insisted on taking me home after the show, but I don't think he realised what he was letting himself in for. To a city slicker like him, the ten-mile drive to Beecroft must have seemed like a trek to the great outback. Nevertheless, he seemed willing to get used to the distance, as he soon became a frequent guest in our house - almost a part of the family. We two became a mutual admiration society: I admired his undoubted abilities as a deejay while he encouraged me in my fight for originality. Our friendship grew strong enough to survive throughout both our eventful lives and remains to this day.

The Sydney Stadium show not only marked a watershed in my relationship with Dad, it also established public recognition of my changing musical identity. However, though it was a step in the right direction, I felt the need for something with more dynamics. My drive for individuality demanded that my route should take me where few had gone before.

I Remember Me

-11-

COLOUR ME GREEN

The invitation was innocuous enough: "Please attend a TV screen test at 1.15pm, on the 6th September 1956 at St David's Hall in Arthur Street, Surry Hills."

I knew nothing of television. Television wasn't even in its infancy in Australia. It was yet to be born and I, chosen to act as one of its midwives, was to attend its birth. I was certainly flattered - there was something creatively challenging about the potential of this new media and I was highly excited by the prospect of appearing on it.

I tried to glimpse as many as I could of the unscheduled test programmes and newscasts that could be seen in shop windows, but even so, I had no idea of what was in store for me when Mum and I stepped through the door of the rustic church hall.

It was like entering a time warp and I felt it was almost blasphemy that this former old church building should have been so unceremoniously transformed into a mass of snaking black cables, banks of lights and flickering screens, with giant cameras lumbering among them like creatures from outer space. I was trying to take it all in, when a tall man strode towards us beneath a huge white Stetson. He introduced himself in a pronounced drawl, as Lofty Coalston. He had come to Australia from America to instruct us greenhorns in the art of producing a Country Music TV show.

I had to leave Mum talking with him, because I was suddenly whisked away into a chair for makeup. This was a horrifying experience, for they were experimenting on me with green lipstick and dark blue mascara and eyeliner, in an attempt to achieve natural skin tones for this new black and white medium. The effect was ghastly. Thank goodness there was no audience other than my mum, as I looked like a monster from a Dracula movie. I did however, get a fleeting view of myself on the monitor screen and it looked passable to me. More to the point, it must have been deemed acceptable to all concerned because I was booked to appear.

TCN Channel 9, for whom I had auditioned, had been ready to open for some weeks, but they were obliged to wait until the ABC had caught up. However, TCN were to be the first to broadcast television to the nation and my own show, called *Campfire Favourites*, would become the first musical show ever to appear on Australian TV, at 7.15pm on 16th of September 1956, the opening night.

I arrived at St David's Hall studio in the afternoon to find Lofty already hard at work. This time the atmosphere was far more intense. The set, a studio mock-up of a camp fire, was ready and I got straight down to rehearse my songs. The quarter hour show had a simple format, featuring me with my guitar, accompanied by the accordion of Alf Luciani and Gordon Scott on violin. When the time got close, we took our positions around the 'camp fire', ready to go... 7.15 ticked closer... newsreader Chuck Faulkner was signing off...

"Standby!" said the studio manager and his fingers went down one at a time as he counted " 5 4 3 2... You're on the air."

I moved quickly into action, strumming a train rhythm while Alf's fingers flew over the keys and buttons and Gordon, with resin flying off his bow, got down to some furious fiddling. The camera picked up each of us in turn, a-pickin' and a-grinnin', until finally it came to rest on Lofty lying prostrate by the campfire, a-chewing at a straw.

"Howdy folks" he drawled "welcome to *Campfire Favourites*"

Then the studio manager signalled to me and off I went with...

Gypsy heart when you hear the whistle of a train....

The show ran like clockwork and we had just reached the last song when I caught the whiff of a strange smell. It was all I could do, not to wrinkle my nose and sniff. I glanced down and was alarmed to see that the plastic 'logs' of our camp fire, scorched by an overheated electric bulb, had started to smoulder. The pretend fire had suddenly become all too real. Soon the hall reeked with the pungent odour, but there was nothing we could do. This was live television and we had to keep going. I struggled through the song somehow, taking in deep gulps of choking fumes with each breath. When finally the credits finished rolling, we all, cameramen and crew included, broke into fits of coughing, gagging desperately for air. Thus ended the first music show on Australian television.

As there was no immediate audience feedback, I had to wait until I got home to find out how I'd fared. My family had driven to Eastwood to watch the show through the window of the TV retail store where other families of the neighbourhood had joined them. They were ecstatic in their reaction and particularly liked the camera close-up on *Unchained*

I Remember Me

Melody - "It was so close, we could see right up your nose!" my brothers quipped.

These early shows are celebrated now as something of a landmark in television, but at the time, I don't think any of us realised we were creating history. Throughout the show's thirteen-week run, it was a case of the blind leading the blind. We tentatively experimented with format and presentation, while each of us learned the trade. Today, these shows might seem amateurish and rough round the edges, but the technology was primitive then and the lack of video recording equipment meant everything had to be broadcast live. It was a case of living on your wits. Also, there were so many new rules to remember - not to wear stripes or white; not to make sudden moves or stretch your arms towards the camera; to be aware at all times of positioning yourself within set boundaries. It's a wonder it turned out as successfully as it did.

The proof of success was, however, self-evident. By November, I had become a leading light in television, with my experience - such as it was - in great demand. Soon, I was being flown to do TV shows in Melbourne, such as HSV Channel 7's *Sunny Side Up* featuring two of Australia's perennial comedians, Sid Heylen and Max Reddy. Here, I sang duets with Max's attractive young daughter, Helen, who, in the fullness of time, moved to America and found international fame with her hits *Angie Baby* and *I Am Woman*.

Along with my fellow artistes Col Joye, The Deltones and John Laws, I joined the first of a television series called *Bandstand* that took to the screen in December and went on to become one of the most memorable and long running shows in Australia. It was a more ambitious variety show compered by Brian Henderson, later to become TV's perennial newscaster. One evening, Brian was taken ill at the very last moment. With little preparation, I was thrust in front of the cameras as the anchorman. I thought I made quite a good job of it considering, but I must say I was even more impressed with Brian's rapid powers of recovery. Could it have been because I did such a good job? Or maybe because I was so bad? I never did find out.

Although television was giving me a high profile in the business, it reached only a minority of homes in those days, so I still had to get out and about to gain a wider audience. Shows of the calibre of the Sydney Stadium were few and far between and it was the one-night stands in clubs and smaller venues that became the bread and butter of my existence. However, through TV and appearances in top class shows, I'd learned the importance of good lighting. So, as the budding producer, I hit on the bright idea of owning my own spotlight.

It was an unwieldy thing, taking up the entire back seat of my Ford Zephyr. Therefore, whoever was my passenger - my brother or any friend who would work for nothing - inherited the job of being my lighting operator. The rest of the show worked in whatever was the available lighting in the room, but when I was announced the spot-lamp swung into action and - Zap! - I was flooded in a sudden burst of brilliant light, a real star turn.

It wasn't always a boon - it could sometimes be a curse, as it proved to be one night when I was appearing at a bowling club. I was announced and confidently stepped forward... into instant blackout. Stunned silence was followed by an undercurrent of muttering as people groped for matches so they could find their drinks. Eventually power was restored and I managed to restart, minus my 'star' light.

Afterwards, the manager collared me for a dressing-down. I realised the sudden power surge from my spotlight had overloaded the venue's electrical circuit and I guessed what was coming - a justified homily on the dangers in which I'd placed the public and the damage to his premises. In truth, though, the full extent of the calamity was much greater than I could possibly have imagined. Like an erupting volcano, he exploded over me:

"Bloody disaster. That spotlight of yours has knocked out the pumps. WE'VE GOT NO BEER!"

♪♫♪♫♪

In those days, a popular outing was to cruise Sydney's magnificent harbour on a paddlewheel showboat, whilst being entertained by a variety show. The *Kalang* was the best known of these and featured many of Australia's top performers on its shows. I'd first played the *Kalang* just after my appearance on *Amateur Hour* and for many years had regular spots on Mondays, Wednesdays and Saturdays.

One Saturday, Janet, a dear friend of ours and a frequent visitor to our house, arrived to join our John and his friends for an evening out at the drive-in movies. I was just leaving for my show on the *Kalang*.

"Goodbye Frank," she said.

"Goodbye Janet," I replied, kissing her lightly on the cheek.

"May your future be all that you could wish for."

"Why, thank you," I said, puzzled. It sounded so final, as though she expected never to see me again and I couldn't for the life of me understand why.

Kalang showboat cruising Sydney harbour

The show started normally enough. The crowd was warm and appreciative and I was just settling into my performance when an overwhelming feeling of foreboding welled up inside me. It was bizarre. I could sense that something was dreadfully wrong, yet had no idea what it could possibly be. Eventually, shaking uncontrollably, I had to leave the stage.

Mr Flockhart, the cruise director, approached, took me to one side and informed me he had received an urgent call concerning a fatal accident involving my brother John. Fortunately John had escaped with a badly broken leg, but his companion Janet had died.

How had she known she was about to be taken away from us? I knew she was a religious girl having been a Sunday school teacher, so maybe instinctively she heard God calling her. What's more, how did I foresee that something terrible had happened? Had she somehow managed to reach me in her last moments? I may never know the answer, but I do know her image would frequently come to mind in times when I felt in need of confidence and I would recall her words of encouragement and the faith she had in me.

Colour Me Green

I don't know if this supernatural encounter had opened my mind to such things, but a short while later, early in the new year of 1958, I experienced yet another premonition that came this time in a dream. I screamed so loudly that my family rushed to my room to discover what was amiss – but the nightmare was too vivid, real and terrible to relate and I couldn't tell them, for it involved us all. I would have been even more terrified had I known my nightmare was about to come true.

The following Sunday was the first in a long while when I wasn't working and for once I was free to spend the day with my family. Dad, being so delighted we were all at home together, suggested we go out for the day, to picnic in the Blue Mountains around Picton. We agreed wholeheartedly with his plan and there was a great deal of excitement as everyone clambered into two cars – my Ford Zephyr and Dad's new Oldsmobile Rocket 88. My passengers were Gran, Robert, Colin and John, whose leg was still in plaster after his accident. In Dad's car were Mum, Jim, David, his friend George and our youngest brother, Philip.

I led the way as we left Sydney's suburbs and headed for the hills with their promise of cool, mountain air. We were driving at a leisurely pace along the steep twisting roads, my father's car contentedly following mine, when, on a narrow winding pass near Picton, Dad suddenly decided to shoot past me. I was surprised and wondered at his hurry. His car hurtled on into the next hairpin bend, travelling far too fast to make the turn. In numb horror, I saw the car, Dad and passengers hurtle over the edge of the cliff and disappear from view.

I pulled my car to a halt in a screech of rubber, leapt out and rushed to the side of the precipice. Gritting my teeth, I forced myself to look over the edge. Two hundred feet below, down in a gully, I saw the mangled remains of my father's car. There was no movement and no sound. The shrill echo of my scream pierced the unnatural silence.

Shouting a desperate appeal for God's help, I tumbled down those cliffs like an avalanche, stumbling, jumping, falling and tearing my flesh on the dense undergrowth which seemed intent on barring my way. I landed on my knees at the bottom of that terrible descent where, dazed and winded, I struggled to my feet.

From somewhere close at hand, I could hear my father moaning. I looked around and noticed that he had climbed out of the wreckage and was sitting on a rock, dazed and delirious, with his head on his knees. Jim was wandering around with a nasty gash in his leg but seemed totally oblivious of his own injuries as he limped to offer assistance to others. David and Philip had been flung from the car into the river and were

I Remember Me

being brought ashore by some helpful people who had been swimming there. Both boys were far too motionless for my liking. I caught sight of young George who, apart from his bewilderment, was totally unharmed and I took some hope from that... but where was my mother? She was nowhere to be seen! I crawled around the upturned vehicle, searching... and there she was. My MUM! Trapped and bleeding! I took her hand to comfort her, while she bravely uttered:

"I'll be alright. Don't worry about me... but where is Philip?"

I remember saying that everyone was OK, but she knew somehow that something was desperately wrong with our Philip. Robert was with us now, trying to ease her concerns. Dad was still moaning in his delirium. Mum could hear him and defying her own agony, called her encouragement to him:

"You mustn't die now dear, we all need you."

At last, John returned after contacting the hospital and managed to hobble down with the ambulance men. They took our family to Camden hospital, although later Mum was moved to Ryde hospital for specialist major surgery to her badly injured shoulder. Both David and Philip had suffered dreadful head injuries and remained in a coma.

The house never felt emptier than it did that night when we returned home. Gran took Mum's place in the running of the household and was a tower of strength to us all, as we supported each other through this crisis.

After what seemed a lifetime, David stirred and regained consciousness - but not so our beloved Philip, who remained asleep as he passed into God's hands. Mum's intuitive concern had been tragically vindicated. Because they were both still in hospital, Mum and Dad weren't able to attend the funeral of their youngest child, and Robert and I reflected on the extra heavy cost this must have been to them.

We rarely refer to the accident, as the memory remains too painful. However, it brought us even closer than before. We often speak of Philip in our conversations, even though it causes eyes to redden and hearts to grieve. I continue to think of my family as being complete and I remain proud to count myself as being one of SEVEN boys.

Subsequently, I learned that the accident happened because the power steering on Dad's car failed which, in turn, caused the pressure servo to the power brakes to become ineffective. However, although I know all that, I still can't help but blame myself for the whole disaster, for if I hadn't been at home that Sunday it might never have happened. It seems strange, on reflection, that the only passenger who was unharmed in the accident was not related to us. It was almost as if this devastating event was meant for our family alone - but why? Furthermore, why was I given an advance insight into this tragedy? I'm still at a loss to understand.

I have not returned to that winding road near Picton. I seem to have formed a mental block to that whole area. Indeed, I dreaded the thought of having to face this horrific time again in writing this account but I have found it to be somehow therapeutic, as I ponder upon a family's strength in adversity and remind myself of the power of a mother's love. Nothing will ever match the strength I witnessed in my mum on that fatal day and may it please God the horror of this experience will never be repeated.

♪♫♪♫♪

It was difficult to go through the motions of normal life during those terrible dark days yet, somehow, it seemed the only way to cope.

I was kept busy with more and more television shows and no doubt it was good for me to have so much work to immerse myself in. I had a new ABC TV series of my own called *Barbecue*, which has become blurred in my memory due to the heaviness of my heart at the time. However, my recollection of the next series is much stronger, owing to the fact that for the first time ever I was to sing in public without my guitar. It was another ABC TV production, *Make Ours Music*, with the Jim Gussey Orchestra.

Technology had advanced sufficiently now for songs to be prerecorded, then mimed on the actual live broadcast. Even so, I found the rehearsal an ordeal. I'd not performed in front of such a large orchestra before and, robbed of the freedom of my own accompaniment, I was overwhelmed by nerves and found difficulty with my timing. It was only due to Neil Williams, who headed the backing singers, that I was able to sing the difficult *Begin the Beguine*. He had physically to cue me into each line and I admit even today I have difficulties with it.

However, as the series progressed, I became more confident and started to enjoy the experience of singing with a full orchestra. I discovered I was stretching my vocal abilities and developing far beyond a mere singer-guitarist into the realms of an all-round singer-performer. I began to feel that maybe those dreams I'd always harboured of appearing on the world stage could possibly be within reach if I widened my ambitions and prepared myself for the next step - but how was I to do it and where was I to go?

America was the obvious move. At that time, Australian artists wishing to extend their horizons were naturally drawn to the USA. Our television was based on the American model, as was our radio; our

I Remember Me

popular music also orientated itself to the American charts - even the majority of our visiting international stars were American.

So why then did I experience an insistent power calling me to England?

Near our house was a golf course, and at night time it had become my favourite place to escape on my own, for walking and pondering on life. Out on its open expanses, I felt near to God and my conversations with Him came as naturally as talking to my family. I laid bare to Him my innermost doubts and ambitions, knowing from past experience I would be granted His guidance if it were meant to be. Where should I go next? I asked, night after night. And as my mind drifted into calm silence, I would feel the answer to my question. It came from a still, small voice in or beyond the ether. Its message was clear and always the same: I should return to England.

Although I'd been given my answer, I still faced a quandary. To go back to England meant parting from everything I held dear. I would have to leave my family and give up my comfortable, sunny, happy and successful life here in Australia. Was I willing to sacrifice it all for the sake of my ambition? And what if I failed?

Ultimately the choice of whether to go or stay would have to be mine. Man has inherited the power of free will in order to be master of his own destiny, yet the wisdom to choose the right path only comes with faith, which I had, and experience of life, which I was too young to have acquired. Still, I'd lived long enough to know that fortune waits to favour those who are brave enough to confront its challenges. God is omniscient in wisdom and love. I'd asked Him for his guidance and He had given me His answer. It would be sheer folly to disregard His counsel and I would do so at my own risk. His love for us is eternal, so what on earth did I have to fear?

Out there on the golf course, I came to a monumental decision. Since England was ordained as the 'way to go', then go I must. Yet the future still remained a large grey uncertainty - I might well be master of my own destiny but I didn't know when and I couldn't envisage how I was going to be able to fulfil it.

-12-

HEY WORLD – HERE I AM

My destiny chose to personify itself in the guise of a man called Peter Gormley. Unheralded, he walked into my life at the ABC studio from where I was doing a regular weekly TV show called *Make Mine Country Style*. He barred my exit with an obvious intent that stopped me in my tracks. I met his gaze; one eye regarded me straight and true while the other skewed off over my shoulder. I was on my guard immediately. What could this stranger with the shifty squint want of me?

I soon found out, for he didn't mince words. He introduced himself, trapped me in the grip of his handshake and asked "Would you like me to be your manager?"

What was I to say? This required a businesslike approach, since I didn't want to give the idea I was ripe for easy pickings.

"What experience do you have?" I asked, finally.

"Well, currently I'm the manager of Hoyt's cinema in Wagga Wagga," he said, which didn't seem overly relevant to the management of an artist. "But I've not come here to stand around singing my own praises. I'll tell you this though - I could be the making of you. I can take your career way beyond the confines of Australia into realms you've only dreamed of. There's just one condition though. If you accept my offer you must be prepared to uproot and go with me to England."

England? I stood, gob-smacked. It was as if he could read my mind, as though he were somehow privy to my intimate deliberations on the golf course. I needed time to think and also needed some parental advice.

"I'm certainly interested in your offer, Mr Gormley. But first, you must realise I'm not yet twenty-one, therefore you will need to put your proposal to my parents for their approval."

We made a date for him to come to my home to meet Mum and Dad. He took his leave with yet another handshake, tipped his hat and disappeared as suddenly as he'd come, while I was left to ponder on what on earth was happening.

Peter's ring on the doorbell was dead on the appointed hour. He was dressed in a sober business suit and tie and I caught the glint of approval in Dad's eye as they shook hands. Dad was a shrewd judge of character, having had many years' experience in appointing and training teams of engineers. I knew I could depend on him to make an accurate assessment of Peter.

I Remember Me

Sitting straight-backed on the edge of his chair, Peter unlocked his briefcase, behind which I saw him surreptitiously pop a few aspirin while shuffling his papers. However, his voice was level and confident as he detailed the plans he had for me, making no attempt to hide the difficulties and risks involved and being entirely open about his personal ambitions. Dad paced around the room, interjecting pertinent questions.

After a discrete interval, Mum entered with a tray of afternoon tea. She has a way of putting everyone at ease and soon Peter relaxed, sipping tea from the best china while she studied him from behind her smile. Mum had proved to be a very capable manager for me so far and was used to dealing with people in the business. However, she'd be very wary of handing over her boy to the care of a stranger, and I knew I could rely on her intuitive reaction.

"Well?" I asked, after he had gone.

"No nonsense there," was Dad's verdict. "A straightforward businessman with a good grasp of the practicalities. I'd be happy to give him my trust. He's got drive. He'll go far."

So far, so good. I turned to Mum.

She frowned, looked me up and down and took both my hands in hers. Her face burst into a great round smile. "It sounds wonderful, dear. He seems a well-mannered, caring man. You go with him, if that's what you want."

If that's what I want? Was it? A flood of confusion swept over me. Dad must have felt it too.

"The decision's yours now, son."

What was wrong with me? I'd already accepted England was where I must go, but... it was all happening too quickly... it was too sudden... I wasn't ready... But Peter had come along right on cue, as if sent by Divine design as the catalyst to achieve my goal. If I didn't go now...

I decided to go for it.

So in August 1958, Peter Gormley became my manager. He had chosen me as the means to achieve his own ambitions and I don't mean that to sound callous. There was no doubt his desire to further my career was genuinely sincere and indeed, it was extremely flattering that he recognised in me sufficient talent to enable us both to succeed in our separate spheres. So it was to be a partnership of mutual benefit in which he would groom me for stardom, while gaining through me the experience of show business management he needed to fulfil his own ambitions.

Hey World – Here I Am

However, it wasn't an easy relationship at the start. Peter was much older than me, we had little in common apart from our shared goal and sometimes we clashed over how best to achieve it. I'd been accustomed to doing things my own way, whereas to Peter I was a commodity, his to shape and refine at will. He demanded I follow his direction, not just in business matters but in my song material, presentation and even how I should maintain my image off stage. Occasionally, I would rebel against being so manipulated and there were times when the friction between us made me doubt the wisdom of my decision.

Peter Gormley became my manager in 1958

Fortunately, as we got to know one another better, attitudes began to mellow. He appreciated I needed freedom of self-expression in order to perform at my best, while I, for my part, listened to his advice – though that was not to say I always agreed. I confess it was a relief not to have to concern myself with negotiations, contracts, money and the internal politics of the business. It allowed me more time to concentrate on new ideas and styles, researching, learning, rehearsing and perfecting my act, which was rapidly becoming much more polished and sophisticated. This was a development watched over with some dismay by my fans.

Over the years, I had built up a large and loyal following who loved the Country music and folk songs I had always sung to my solo guitar. Now these were gradually disappearing from my act and there were mutterings I couldn't ignore. I tried explaining my need to progress, but this only alienated them more and I felt like a traitor. To make matters worse, rumours I was leaving Australia began to circulate – and although this was our ultimate plan, at this early stage, I could neither confirm nor deny anything. The fans' worst fears were compounded when, in fact, I did leave to go overseas - to New Zealand.

The offer had come in originally before Peter arrived on the scene. I'd been invited to represent Australia in a big Festival of the Arts tour that was

I Remember Me

to be a showcase for all forms of music from folk to jazz and pop to opera. It was an honour to be asked to appear with a talented array of New Zealand's finest orchestras, operatic singers and ballet dancers plus many other artistes. Yet when I learned I'd be expected to perform in every show, whatever the format, I found the prospect far too daunting even to consider.

Peter, on the other hand, leapt at it.

"What do you mean, you've turned it down? It's precisely what you need," he exclaimed.

"But I don't feel ready for it. It's so completely different from anything I've ever attempted before."

"Exactly! What better opportunity is there to test out this new versatility you've been trying to achieve? It's in a country where you're not so well known and an ideal preparation for England, where very few will know of you at all."

Off to New Zealand with singer Margaret Day.
My gran came to the airport to wish us well

Hey World – Here I Am

It was true. Although I'd had some record success in New Zealand, I was unknown as a live performer there. And yes, he was right, I had been concentrating my efforts on improving my versatility - though not to the extent this tour would require. I was no less daunted by the idea than I had been originally, but Peter was adamant. He confirmed the offer and I was booked to go.

I'd believed I was already working hard, but now fear added extra frenzy to my preparations. Fortunately, help was at hand. Jazz singer Margaret Day was to represent Australia with me, and what a heroine she turned out to be. She encouraged me to put down my guitar and attempt some standards and traditional jazz songs, teaching me syncopation and phrasing with the band.

Ready or not, the day of departure for New Zealand arrived. As this was such an important landmark in my career, Mum bought me a diary so I could record the events of the trip. It started off in fine form...

> **18th February 1959**: *Margaret and I arrived in Auckland this evening after a pleasant trip. We went to the Central Hotel where they informed us that they knew nothing of the booking and that they, along with every other hotel in the city, were booked up. So here we are now, holed up in the hotel lounge. Margaret is trying hard to sleep while I am writing this entry in my diary and falling into a stupor. Why does this happen to us? The lounge chairs are too small... and hard.*

> **19th February 1959**: *Arrived in New Plymouth to be greeted by a public relations officer who informed us that the organiser Mr Hanbury was down with the 'flu and everything was in turmoil. We had lunch and met New Zealand's rock star Johnny Devlin. Then we were whizzed off to the local radio station for a round of interviews to be followed by a rehearsal - I was quite pleased with the band and hope the show tomorrow will be a good one. Look out bed - here I come.*

> **20th February 1959**: *Today was most uneventful - bleak and wet. Due to the rain our first show was cancelled, but we will appear tomorrow night to do the Variety show that should have been on tonight.*

That was the third and final entry. Short though these extracts may be, they do reveal my first exposure to the chaos and confusion that is typical of tours like these. If my diary had continued, it would have told of

I Remember Me

a whirlwind of events, taking in the Festival of Wellington and all the other major towns. We hardly stopped to take a breath, because, sandwiched in between all these live shows, we recorded eleven radio shows for NZBC.

It was hell, but I survived through to the final concert at the Brooklands Bowl in New Plymouth. Now, this was the occasion that had scared me stiff from the very start. It was a special night, dedicated mainly to Opera. How was I, a glorified Country singer, going to perform in front of an audience of opera lovers? I wasn't a great opera lover, but I did admire Mario Lanza and Enzio Pinza, so therefore I chose the drinking song from *The Student Prince* and *Some Enchanted Evening* from *South Pacific*. To finish, I decided on, what was a bold move in the circumstances, Peter Dawson's New Zealand Maori song *Waita-Poi* - the very song I used to play on Gran's wind-up gramophone when I was a young lad in England. I gave it my best shot - I could do no more - and to my great relief, they liked it.

Though I cursed him for it, I had to admit that Peter was right to insist I went. I'd learned how to live on my nerves and cope in an unfamiliar environment; I'd been forced to extend the breadth of my musical knowledge way beyond its limit; I'd proved my ability to win over an audience who didn't know me. The added bonus was a newly gained confidence. I felt like shouting from the treetops, "Watch out England, I'm ready for you!"

I might well have thought so, but Peter didn't agree, because when I got home, I found he had an overloaded schedule lined up for me. He seemed determined to cram a lifetime's experience into the last few months remaining to me in Australia.

Time disappeared fast in a blur of cabaret, radio and television. I found among Mum's souvenirs a cutting from the June 20th 1959 edition of Australia's leading television magazine *TV Week* and have taken the liberty of reproducing part of it here, because Peter McDonald sums up perfectly just how hectic life was.

> *Last Saturday night Frank appeared at Romano's and sang such songs as 'You Do Something To Me' and 'Old Black Magic'. On Monday night he rehearsed 'Oklahoma' for ABN 2's 'Make Ours Music'. Wednesday morning he recorded 'Jedda' and 'Come Softly To Me' for ABC's Saturday night variety program 'Roundabout'. That night he appeared in 'Make Ours Music' and then dashed across to ATN7 to compere 'Cue for Music' in which he sang 'Begin The*

Beguine'. He was at the Australia Hotel singing with Sid Simpson's band and on Friday recorded four special 15 minute shows for ABC.

When Peter Gormley left for England in the July of 1959 to prepare for my coming, it set the seal of inevitability on the whole enterprise. There was an air of finality over everything I did from now on, as my shows began to acquire the prefix of 'farewell' or 'last'. One of these 'lasts' was also a notable debut - my first LP.

I'd been issuing records continuously from the time of my first release back in 1953 but, since I didn't consider myself a pop artist, I'd never had an eye on the record charts. However, Peter Gormley saw it differently. Early on in our partnership, he'd negotiated with EMI to move me from Regal Zonophone to the more prestigious Columbia label and had introduced me to a prolific songwriter named Laine Goddard. She wrote a song for me called *True* that was an adaptation of the main theme from Tchaikovsky's ballet *Swan Lake*. Not only was it a complete change for me, but the musical arrangement by Don Burrows, melding a classic theme with rock and roll, was totally unique for the times. The record became my very first pop chart entry.

This had opened the way to an LP called *Yours Sincerely*, covering a wide variety of material from country to jazz; it was to complete the recording of this LP that I was in the studios for my final Australian recording session.

Sensing that I might be a bit depressed, my brothers trouped along to the studios to lend moral support. Now the trouble is when we all get together, you can never be sure quite what will happen.

During one of the breaks, we were fooling around together when Christmas was mentioned. I sat down with a bump, struck by a sudden melancholy. All of this would still be here at Christmas - the studios, the musicians, the engineers, my brothers - only I wouldn't.

"Hey, what's up with you?"

"Christmas," I muttered.

"Christmas? What do you mean 'Christmas'?"

"I won't be here. I'll be missing you all dreadfully, especially Mum."

So my brothers suggested I record a special song for her as a present. I brightened immediately at this. But what song? Then I had it - an even better idea.

"Why don't we all do a song together? That would really be special. Let's record *Anna Marie* just for her."

I Remember Me

Anna Marie was a song we'd performed on one of my television appearances in *Bandstand*. Our Colin had taken lead vocals, while John, Robert and myself sang the harmonies. It had been something of a personal triumph for Colin. He'd received such enthusiastic audience response that he'd been persuaded to appear on another television show, Johnny O'Keefe's *Sing-sing-sing*.

For a few years, Colin did pursue a solo career and would probably have become a star had it not been for me. When I finally became a success overseas, he grew weary of always having to sing my songs and not his own, so sadly he gave it up to concentrate on engineering. But *Anna Marie* by the Ifield Brothers did see the light of day when it was issued later as a coupling to one of my recordings.

Speculation about my departure was rife. I was constantly being pressed to reveal the date of my leaving, but I couldn't say; I was still waiting for Peter in England to suggest the right time. Meanwhile, my silence was creating a backlash of counter-rumours that maybe nothing had materialised overseas and I didn't really intend leaving Australia after all. I was in danger of being thought a failure before I'd even tried.

Bombarded by what my father once called 'the abominable no men', even I began to give some credence to the rumours, and was starting to have doubts myself. Then I reflected upon the words of a man I admired for his own strength in adversity - ace-guitarist George Gollah, who had learned to play his instrument while totally bed ridden in hospital. At my last recording session, George had said "Go for it Frank - you've got what it takes."

I simply couldn't afford to wait any longer.

It was Dad who came up with the date. He suggested I leave in style on the inaugural Comet flight to London - the first jet propelled passenger flight between Australia and Britain. The event could prove to be good publicity for me. Yet more significantly, how appropriate it was that I - R. J. Ifield's son - should set out in my bid to gain fame and recognition as the first paying passenger transported by the very technology that had been the shining success of my father's own career.

The flight was scheduled for departure on the 4th of November 1959.

Stiff upper lip was the order of the day. My entire family and many relatives and friends had gathered to see me off at Mascot Airport. There I stood - the centre of attention in my hat and brand new pin stripe suit with specially tailored cuffs on its sleeves. Outwardly I appeared composed, except for the telltale fumbling as I searched for my passport and documents.

The entire family came to send me off to England.
Left to right: Colin, Gran, David, John, me, Robert, Mum, Jim, Dad

"Have you got your hanky?" enquired Gran, as she had always done whenever she felt emotional or lost for words.

"We'll all miss you dear. Make sure you have enough to eat and wrap up warm," Mum instructed, bravely trying to stave off her tears.

"Now don't forget son, you'll be absolutely safe in the Comet. Always look for the RR emblem and you'll know my fuel pumps are fitted to it," Dad said in his matter-of-fact manner.

Breathing deeply to regain my composure, I struggled to find a word for each of my brothers. "Robert, you are going to sell my Ford Zephyr aren't you and any other bits and pieces I may have left behind? Good luck with your singing career Colin, I'll be watching the Australian charts for your name. Jim, I'll send you postage stamps for your collection from every foreign place I visit. John, I know you've always longed to travel so maybe I'll be seeing you over there soon. And David, goodbye you cheeky monkey, always keep your unique sense of humour. I miss you all already and I'm not even gone... what I mean is... what I wanted to say was..."

My speech faded until finally it was gagged by the lump in my throat - but there was no time for more, anyway, as they had called the flight. After a round of hugs, kisses and cheerios from my many well-wishers, it was a quick wave and I was gone, wending my solitary way across the

I Remember Me

tarmac, clutching at my flight-bag while summoning the courage to board that streamlined jet.

Seated on board, I felt overwhelmed by the sheer enormity of the step I was taking. In those days, Australia was much more distant than it is today, now flights are commonplace and communication instant. Back then, I'd no idea when I'd next be able to speak to my family, let alone see them again.

I was making a tremendous sacrifice in my quest for fame and, now there was no turning back, I became engulfed in waves of insecurity and doubts. What in the hell was I doing? Was it really worth it? What made me think I had something to offer the people of Great Britain? Would God still find me 13,000 miles away? Where would I live? Who would I know? What if it all went wrong? How would I survive without my mum?

Suddenly the mighty thrust of the engines launched us like a rocket, zooming into the unfathomable blue of the Sydney sky. I could but watch as everything I held dear flashed away below... and quietly, I began to sob.

- 13 -

UP, DOWN AND AWAY

The best way to describe the flight is to say it was like riding the Big Dipper - fun for a few minutes maybe, but for hour after hour? We changed pilots at every stop and each new avid aviator appeared more determined than the last to put her through her paces. Even as I write, memories come flooding back of waves of nausea, dizziness and the G-force exerted on my body and pressure in my ears while they indulged their compunction to fly her as fast and as vertically as she could manage without stalling.

After another hair-raising landing, we were unceremoniously deplaned onto the tarmac of Dubai. I staggered around the airport like a zonked out zombie, until suddenly my eyes were dragged out of their sockets at the sight of an unabashed nude. She smiled alluringly at me in glorious living colour from the cover of a glossy American magazine called *Playboy*. I stood transfixed, staring with my mouth agape.

"How disgustingly brazen," I thought, for up until that moment I had unknowingly been sheltered from such decadence.

In those days, Australia was subject to strict censorship laws and I had accepted this public moral code without question. I'd always considered the Sydney lifestyle to be cosmopolitan and worldly. Suddenly I was made to feel like an unsophisticated hick from the backwoods.

The shock had the effect of stimulating me out of my lethargy and I vowed to make a start on my education. When the call came to embark, I made my way to the line self-consciously clutching a carefully rolled up souvenir. In the privacy of my solitary seat I took out my purchase and chanced a peek. The remainder of the journey passed more quickly whilst I furtively engrossed myself in close scrutiny of this provocative publication.

Unlike all the previous stops the landing at Heathrow, London, was simply superb. We glided in and touched down with feather-light precision in the mist of an early November evening.

I wondered at the blaze of rockets and fireworks that had greeted us until something about the significance of the date penetrated my mind from my distant English childhood. "Remember, remember the 5th of November, gunpowder, treason and plot" went the rhyme, and indeed it was the fifth of November – Guy Fawkes Night, 1959. The English were celebrating the thwarting of a plot to blow up Parliament three and a half centuries earlier. Memories came flooding back of when I was a young lad constructing a 'Guy' from old clothes stuffed with newspapers and parading him around the streets in a pram, begging 'a penny for the Guy', and it was a timely reminder to me that this English-born Aussie was indeed returning to the land of his birth.

I got up from my seat, straightened my tie, flicked back my fly-away hair, flattened the creases in my suit as best I could, and joined the line of passengers in a follow-my-leader procession through Her Majesty's Customs. Then out into - where? I stretched up on tip-toe in search of a friendly face.

"G'day Frank" came a familiar twang from beneath a broad-brimmed hat, making me feel I had never left Australia. It belonged to Peter Gormley.

"How was your trip?" he asked; then without waiting for a reply he grabbed my arm. "Come this way Frank, I've got... bloody hell! What on earth are these?" He'd noticed the cuffs on my sleeves. "You shouldn't have had those put on - they'll think them a bit hick over here." Before I could open my mouth to answer, he was off again. "Whatever you do, do not volunteer any information, or answer any questions without checking with me first."

I was in no fit state to argue. More than forty sleepless hours in a cramped seat had left me in a grimy, crumpled stupor. All I wanted was to slink off to a comfortable billet where I could crash out and forget everything until my mind caught up with my body and I could think straight again. Yet here was Peter dragging me purposefully across a crowded terminal, criticising my attire, and mumbling about information and questions. What the hell was going on?

My bleary eyes could just about discern a crowd of photographers standing expectantly, and I wondered who they were waiting for. Suddenly, I was aware of a hand being offered to me and, on a reflex, I shook it.

Immediately, I was caught up in a blaze of flashing lights that made me think the fireworks had followed me inside. I lifted my gaze from the hand, up the arm, and onto a mouthful of white teeth set in a broad grin. Even in my befuddled state, I recognised him - yes, I was staring directly into the friendly face of Tommy Steele.

Up, Down and Away

Arriving in England after a 40 hour Comet flight from Sydney, looking fresher than I felt.

I Remember Me

So that was what it was all about. A press conference - for me! And, what's more, with one of Britain's favourite singing stars. I knew I could rely on Peter to have been doing some sterling work on my behalf, but he had excelled himself. This was indeed starting at the top.

In my jet-lagged condition, I had no idea what questions were being asked, let alone what my replies were. The only answer I recall giving, and this was definitely without seeking Peter's approval, was to a pretty pair of come-hither eyes belonging to a junior reporter. Her question concerned a private interview later in my hotel room. My answer was brief, but positive.

Conference over, I could think only of escaping, and I hoped silently that Peter would make our excuses and lead the way out. But it was not to be. Tommy had waited behind and was now inviting me to a Bonfire Night Party. I had no choice but to go - as he apparently had organised it in my honour.

I couldn't help but like Tommy. His cockney cheerfulness was infectious and soon had me believing that to sleep would be a wicked waste of time. Besides, I was conscious of the tempting pair of eyelashes, fluttering like butterflies at my elbow. I remember thinking: "Well, if I am going to a party, then I may as well enjoy it," so I offered my arm as her escort.

I was vaguely aware of Peter muttering something while setting flame to a cigarette, but I took no notice of him until, after a long relaxing draw, he pronounced, "I suppose we do need to establish your sex appeal, but you certainly didn't waste any time in confirming it."

After the party, of which I remember very little, we returned to the stylish Park Lane hotel near Marble Arch where Peter had a room booked for me. Here my escort acquired her private interview... and so, at last, to sleep...

The following morning came all too soon for my confused internal clock to register. However, with the help of a shower to stimulate a flicker of life in my aching body, I was able to join Peter for a hearty English breakfast. He was already sitting at the table and his "Good morning Frank" came out from behind a large newspaper.

"Good m..." I started, but he'd already begun reading aloud:

"Last night Tommy Steele, who makes his down-under debut next February, acted as host at a 'Welcome to Britain' party in London for top recording artist Frank Ifield... "

I picked up a second newspaper and stumbled on another piece, which I muffled out through a mouth full of cold buttered toast.

"Mr Steele and friends were waiting to welcome Frank Ifield, an Australian singer born in Coventry. He arrived wearing a weary smile and a suit with turned-back cuffs."

"I knew it! Those bloody cuffs!" Peter grabbed the paper to read for himself. Later, warmed by the coffee, he admitted that perhaps the cuffs hadn't been such a bad idea after all, for they did warrant an extra paragraph in the press. Nevertheless, I rarely wore that suit again.

♪♫♪♫♪

There's a lot of truth in the old adage 'after the Lord Mayor's show comes the muck cart', for, having wallowed in the luxury of the Park Lane Hotel for the sum total of one night, I was shunted off into the dingy back streets behind Victoria station.

As we splashed along through the puddles, it wasn't just the cold of a late English autumn that made me shiver; it was the uncertainty of the future. By the time we reached our destination and were trudging up the bare boards of the stairway, I was beginning to doubt the wisdom of giving up my sunny Sydney life for this. Peter unlocked the door. It creaked open and I fumbled my way into what can only be described as the grim cell of a condemned man.

When my eyes became accustomed to the gloom, I saw my suitcase and guitar were standing on a threadbare rug in the middle of a room no bigger than my bedroom at home, a small bed-sit representing the entire living quarters for the two of us. The furniture looked like the unsold rejects of a jumble sale, while the 'kitchen' boasted a cracked sink, a grease-stained gas-hob, and a water heater rescued from the galley of Noah's Ark. The place shuddered with the passing steam-trains as they shunted and snorted to and fro below the window, adding a taste of coal dust to the aroma of stale cooking and cigarette smoke that permeated the room. In an attempt to dispel the gloom, Peter flicked on the light switch, but the bulb produced only a faint yellow glow, which did little to brighten my mood.

Some time later, after I'd unpacked and Peter had explained the mysteries of the shilling-devouring device called a gas meter, we huddled over our mugs of coffee, trying to find the extra warmth that the gas fire miserably failed to provide. Carefully, I positioned a picture of my family in pride of place on the mantelpiece, and sat back, gazing at it longingly. Oh, how I missed them - especially Mum.

I Remember Me

We have a lot in common, Mum and I, for I've inherited her mouth, nose and eyes and, fortunately, it seems she's passed on to me her perennial good health. I hope, too, I have her bonhomie for rarely is anybody so instantly acceptable to strangers; people take to her instinctively. Most of all, God willing, I hope I have something of her patience and strength to face whatever lies ahead.

I took out my pen and steeled myself to write a cheerful letter home. Then, emotionally drained, I flopped down on my makeshift bed and fell into a deep sleep where I dreamt I was running naked through green fields. I still vividly recall that image for it became a constantly recurring dream, and I looked forward to my nightly streaking and the release it gave from the claustrophobic concrete jungle in which I felt entrapped. Each morning when I awoke, I'd rush to fling the window wide, bursting to fill my lungs with God's clean air; but instead of savouring that first sweet intake, I choked on the coal fumes that became my daily breath.

To give credit where it's due, Peter had done his preparatory work well, and within the first week, I was at the studios of BBC TV to appear in the top rating *Ted Ray Show*. He also pulled off another coup, an appointment with Norrie Paramor, 'artist and repertoire' (A&R) manager for the Columbia label of EMI Records.

At that time, Norrie was one of the most influential figures in the music industry in Britain. He was the man behind the record success of many giant stars such as Cliff Richard & The Shadows, whose latest hit was *Living Doll* and Michael Holliday, who was currently riding high at number one with *Starry Eyed*. Now my chance had arrived. This could be a wonderful opening, if only I could impress him enough to win a contract.

The man behind the spectacles was not conscious of my studying him while Peter held him in negotiation. He had the air of a fatherly figure, no doubt on account of his maturity, and I felt an instinctive trust in him. He seemed to be more a kindred soul than a businessman, I thought, for it was obvious to me that his chief consideration was 'making music'.

As soon as the talking was finished, he moved over to the piano. It was now my turn. I was treated to the full glow of an amiable smile designed to put me at my ease.

"Right Frank," he said, peering over the rim of his glasses, "now let me hear you sing."

I started somewhat hesitantly, but it was evident that he was in tune with my need for musical expression and I soon relaxed, running through a plethora of songs to give him a wide appreciation of my vocal range, my musical tastes and styling. I was convinced we had established a rapport and

Up, Down and Away

was proved right when, to my joyous relief, he agreed to draw up a two-year contract, and arranged a second meeting to select some recording material.

Even our dingy digs in the back blocks of Victoria were illuminated by the radiance of my spirits that night, but the radiance soon faded in the glare of harsh reality. Those opportunities that came my way so easily in Australia seemed elusive here. Not so long ago, I had been begging for a break from the constant stream of work that had been an exacting test of endurance, yet now here I was praying for a full diary.

There was nothing for it, but for Peter and me to take to the streets. One day it would be Fleet Street in an attempt to get my face in the newspapers; the next, we'd be found in and around the music publishing houses of Denmark Street, as it was essential to be seen there. However, pounding the streets was getting us nowhere. The obvious answer was in good representation from a major agency. Naturally, being ambitious, we targeted the top, and you couldn't aspire to anything higher than the Grade Organisation.

We invaded the reception area of their offices at 235 Regent Street and requested audience with Mr Leslie Grade himself. Not unexpectedly, access was denied. Be that as it may, we weren't about to take 'No' for an answer. Like a couple of boomerangs, we returned day after day but, day after day, the answer was the same. At last, when it began to feel we'd become permanent features of the decor along with the furniture and pot plants, their resistance was exhausted and we were escorted to the office of a Mr Eddie Jarrett.

We were barely through the door when Peter leapt into in top gear, filling Eddie's ears with our well-rehearsed story. As usual, I let him do all the talking. He held the floor, extolling the virtues of myself as a saleable product, pointing out my enormous potential for the British scene based on my previous track record of Australian successes. Then he added that I'd already embarked on a promising recording career with EMI and television appearances for the BBC. I would be prepared to do pantomime and summer season; I was willing to tour; my act was as good for cabaret venues and clubs, as it was for the theatre...

"Yes, yes, I'm sure," butted in Eddie at last, "but does he have marquee value? He isn't known here in England, is he?"

It was the dreaded home truth - even Peter had no answer to that. A deathly hush filled the room, while Peter studied his fingernails and I stared at Eddie.

"I could probably try selling him as Britain's answer to Guy Mitchell."

A thousand firecrackers fizzed and popped inside my head. I sealed my lips and kept my emotion bottled inside, but it took a supreme effort of self-control, for I was seething. What? ME? A Guy Mitchell? Never! I've nothing against Guy Mitchell, but well...! I'd not come all this way to hide behind somebody else's success. I'd be my own answer to Frank Ifield - or nothing. I'd rather live on the streets than give up my ideals...

Then it hit me - at this very moment, such was the state of our affairs that unless we could persuade this man to assist us, living on the streets soon may well be the only option left. It had been a valid suggestion, I supposed, and he had intended no insult. I allowed the red haze to fade from my eyes and I focussed on Eddie again. He was looking from one to the other of us for some hint of enthusiasm. My face must have shown my colours and I began to feel uneasy with Peter's silence.

"Er, not keen I take it? I see. Then, what you need is a hit record and we'll be right behind you."

At this point, even Peter lost his cool. "That's bloody obvious!" he exploded. "If we had a hit record, the whole world would be behind us!"

"Great stuff, Peter," I thought to myself, "you've really blown our chances now."

Eddie just chuckled. However, the meeting was at an end. He rose from his seat and shook our hands. "We'll see what we can do for you," he promised.

We thanked him and left. Our expectations were about as high as the heels on our shoes - flat to the ground and wearing down fast.

♪ ♫ ♪ ♫ ♪

If I'd been granted even the merest inkling of just how tough life was going to be in London, I might have had second thoughts about leaving Sydney. It was bad enough having to accept a return to the bottom of the heap when I had already enjoyed the view from the top. However, I'd known this would be the case and was prepared for another hard climb.

No, far worse was the emptiness of my personal life. In London I knew no one and no one knew me. I walked the crowded streets, yet always felt alone. It was such a contrast to Sydney, where everybody knew me, and friendly people would stop to speak or wave 'g'day'. Forsaken and isolated in a wintry London, 'cold' and 'grey' summed up my world very well. Then to top it all off, with very little work, my money was simply melting away on high rents and the high London cost of living. Times were bleak and I was desperate.

Up, Down and Away

I really was in need of someone to turn to with my problems. I couldn't tell my family back home - I always tried to be as positive as I could in my letters home as the last thing I wanted was that Mum should have cause to worry about me. I had to pour out my troubles to someone, though, and it was to my stock car racing friends, Lorna and Col Dennis, that I confessed all the trials and tribulations of my new life. With a sense of relief I would put pen to paper and despatch all my deep distress in a package to Australia. Such was the closeness of our long-lasting friendship, I knew they would understand.

The only person I knew at all well in London was Peter. However, although we had a close working relationship and were very much dependent on each other career-wise, we did not socialise much together. Maybe this was because of the age gap, or just because we needed our own space, but whatever the reason we respected each other's privacy. In fact, working and living so closely together soon began to put a strain on both of us so, despite our straitened financial circumstances, Peter moved out and left me to continue in the flat on my own.

The saving grace of bed-sit land was the camaraderie between 'inmates'. I began to make many friends among those who, like myself, were living hand to mouth. There was constant laughter over some mishap or other - the charred chops; the green mould decorating the last piece of cheese; the empty gas meter; the best white shirt turned grey at the launderette. And then, on rare occasions when money permitted, we'd venture forth to taste the delights of London's nightlife.

My brightest hope lay in my imminent first record release. It may seem that Eddie Jarrett was stating the obvious in asserting I needed a hit record - but to me it still came as a shock. I'd grown up in an era when success depended absolutely on one's ability to entertain and to attract the acclaim of a live audience. Live performance was the cornerstone of my career and I tended to regard all else as of secondary importance. I'd come to England expecting to establish my name via the medium of live theatre and cabaret as I had in Australia. However, I hadn't realised that the world of Variety I had been hoping to find was dying. I didn't appreciate that stars were no longer created on the stage and fame accorded by audience response; the stage was now occupied by stars of the television screen and a singer's popularity was measured by chart positions and record sales.

Although I always took a lot of care over my recordings, I wasn't that interested in chart success as an end in itself. With my move to England, my views hadn't changed. I was first and foremost an entertainer. A string of

I Remember Me

chart hits and the trappings of a pop star certainly hadn't featured on my agenda.

It wasn't until Eddie had stressed the point that I began to understand just how vital chart success was going to be - it was doubtful I could achieve the stardom I sought without it. This was a hard truth for me to have to face. It called for a complete turnaround in my outlook, but if a hit record was what was demanded, then from now on, all my energies must be concentrated on achieving it.

So when the day arrived for the second meeting with Norrie Paramor at EMI, it was commercialism that was at the forefront of my mind when I settled down with him to choose the songs for my first British single. Norrie had assembled a range of what he thought might be suitable material in the form of demo discs from American and British publishers, and we ploughed through the lot.

Now, I'd never before put hit potential at the top of the list of my priorities when choosing recording material, so I found myself listening to the songs with an unaccustomed ear. I knew the one it had to be, as soon as I heard it.

"That's it! *Lucky Devil!*" I announced confidently.

Norrie was somewhat taken aback. "Well, you do surprise me, Frank. I hadn't thought you'd go for that one. What makes you so sure it's the right song for you?"

The truth is, it didn't exactly strike me as necessarily the right song for me, either - oh, I liked it well enough, but there were more mercenary reasons for my choice than merely my own preference and leanings.

"Well, it has a Country feel which is dead right for my image, but what's more important, it also has obvious commercial viability."

Norrie wasn't so convinced. "Yes, it's a good catchy song, but I'm not absolutely certain there's a market for it here."

"But it's a hit in the States and if, as I believe, it's going into the charts here, then I want to be the one to put it there."

This was my first recording for Norrie and I held him in high regard. After all he had put many artists, including himself, into the British charts - which is much more than I had done at this point in time. And yet here was I, telling him what I thought would be commercial.

Fortunately, Norrie appeared to concede. "OK then, if that's how you feel. Maybe we could change..."

"No. I want it just the way it is."

I could hardly believe what I was saying. It was a complete betrayal of my own high ideals. I had battled so hard to discover my own identity

Up, Down and Away

and prided myself on pushing for my individuality. Nevertheless, originality didn't necessarily count in the race for the charts.

If the overriding importance attached to a hit record had come as something of a surprise to me, then I had been even more dismayed to discover that, even here in Britain, the music industry relied heavily on the American influence. British songs by home-grown artists did not score so well, so to ensure success, local artists were encouraged to make cover-versions of American hits. To produce a straight, unabashed copy like this always did and always will seem like plagiarism to me, but I was learning fast. In my desperate bid to break into the charts I was ready, by my own volition, to compromise my beliefs.

All the same, to do so against Norrie's advice seemed a risky ploy, especially since I hardly knew him and I was still trying to establish a rapport upon which my very future depended. On the other hand, I was not a newcomer to recording, having had several years experience on which to base my ideas. I held firm opinions on what I considered right for me.

Right or wrong, Norrie let me have my way. He booked Ken Jones to do the session and we produced a very creditable copy of Carl Dobkins Jr's *Lucky Devil*. While I could be proud of my performance, I couldn't be proud of myself for the deed. I only hoped that the sacrifice would prove worthwhile.

Lucky Devil was launched in the first month of the new decade. I promoted it in a TV appearance on *Thank Your Lucky Stars* and sang it live on BBC Radio's *Saturday Club*. I watched anxiously for its debut into the charts, and to my great relief it made a showing in the lower regions in late January. Then on February 9th, 1960, as if to represent my age, it stood at number twenty-two, poised for its assault on the Top Twenty. Yet it stalled where it was, then vanished only to reappear magically in April for a further two weeks at number 33. That was all the momentum it could muster, and it finally disappeared without trace.

However, I was delighted my first venture had entered the charts at all. The record's flight to fame may have been brief and hardly enough to establish my name in the public's awareness, but it did serve to kick-start my career. On the strength of its performance, and just in the nick of time before the rent was due, Eddie Jarrett came up with some club dates in Manchester and the North of England. These bookings were still far too thinly scattered throughout the pages of my hitherto blank diary, but at least I would be earning some money.

I packed my bags and headed for the train. Half an hour out from Euston station, the suburbs receded, green fields came into view and I felt

I Remember Me

the stresses of London slipping away as the train sped north. Even under a wintry sky, the countryside captivated me, revealing a hidden gem around every corner – a quaint little village, an ancient stone church nestling in the fold of a hill, a narrow boat negotiating a canal - all of them assuring me that England was not all urban sprawl. When we reached the North, the 'dark satanic mills' flashed quickly by, giving way to rolling moors and, for the finale of my journey, the broad sweep of Morecambe Bay glittered beneath the piling peaks of the Lakeland mountains, white-tipped with snow. I stepped out of the train and breathed in the icy tingle of good, fresh air.

I'd not known what to expect of Barrow-in-Furness, which I'd been told, with a grimace, was a shipbuilding town grimed with heavy industry. What greeted me though, was a gracious town of wide, tree-lined streets, warm sandstone buildings and a friendly voice saying "Ee, lad, make yerself at 'ome."

I knew then how contented I felt in choosing England as my second home.

- 14 -

MOSS AND MAYHEM

I was ready and waiting for my entrance, the curtain was due to rise and I could hear the audience settling into their seats. I stood backstage helplessly chewing my nails, trying to remain calm. It was the opening of my first British tour, and it was proving to be a case of baptism by fire.

The star of the show was Emile Ford, who was riding high after his big hit *What Do You Want To Make Those Eyes At Me For?* Yet with minutes to go before the matinee was due to begin, he'd not arrived, and more importantly, neither had his band, the Checkmates, who were to provide my backing. To say the theatre manager was worried is an understatement - he was panic-stricken. He came to throw himself on our mercy. With a full house waiting for a show out there, it would be a shame to cancel now; the stars were sure to arrive by interval; could we handle the first half between us?

Oh-oh! What to do here? If we refused to go on, which we were well within our rights to do, then it would endanger any future prospects with the agents. I could not afford that. On the other hand, if we went on with a totally unrehearsed show, we all risked embarrassing ourselves in front of the paying public. And what if there were a TV scout or a promoter out there? It might ruin my chances through no fault of my own and I could not afford that either. We held a quick discussion. The showbiz tradition with which we were all imbued won through - the show must go on.

Nothing daunted, we set to - and in the space of a few minutes had devised a complete new running order for the first half. Alan Randall opened the show with his George Formby impersonation. For my act, I accompanied myself on my guitar, with Alan, an accomplished musician, at the piano. I stayed on stage to introduce the then redheaded Kathy Kirby, who had to rely on Alan and me to accompany her. Finally, it was West-Indian balladeer Jimmy Lloyd, who also had to make do with our piano and guitar backing for his act that finished with his unique marathon version of *The Nearness Of You.*

Exhausted, I staggered off stage. Unbelievably, there was still no sign of Emile and the Checkmates - just the poor miserable manager pacing up and down. Desperately he begged us, could we do it all over again for the second half, with different songs?

I Remember Me

With Kathy Kirby at Blackpool in 1964. Earlier in our careers, Kathy and I survived my 'baptism by fire' on tour with Emile Ford.

Moss and Mayhem

We were utterly exasperated. But what alternative was there? In the primitive conditions of Aussie show business I had learnt to draw on my resources to cope with almost anything, but poor Kathy was reduced to tears, unable to go on. So it was left to Alan, Jimmy and me. In the desperately short few minutes of the interval, we raked through our repertoire and each constructed a complete new act for the second half. And then we had to go out in front of the same audience again, an audience who were expectantly awaiting a star act they were never going to see.

We did it - and survived. In fact, it seems that after a public apology had been made, most of the patrons were so well satisfied with the show we had given that only a few asked for a refund. As for me, I slumped into my dressing room armchair for a well-earned rest, glad that the torture was over. But was it? With mounting foreboding, I watched the time tick away to the evening show. Ten minutes to go. Where was Emile? Where were the Checkmates? Five, four... and that familiar cold sweat was upon me again. It was back to plan A, with a hope and a prayer that by interval they would surely arrive.

Thankfully, they did. They were somewhat bemused by the cold welcome they got, for they knew nothing of any arrangements made for them to back the show nor, indeed, that there was a matinee performance at all. I thought nothing more could astonish me that day, but I was wrong - for, to cap it all off, Emile got onto a ladder in full view of the audience and proceeded to put up his own speakers while the band tested his microphone. "1.. 2.. testing.. 1.. 2.."

Well, I sighed to myself, so that's British showbiz, is it?

♪♫♪♫♪

Spring was now on its way, evident in the ripening buds and carpets of crocuses and daffodils blooming in London's squares and parks. Gradually, the city was growing into a warmer place in my heart. This was in no small way due to expatriate Aussie Ron Grainer, composer of the TV themes for *Steptoe and Son, Dr Who, Inspector Maigret* and *That Was The Week That Was*. On one of my infrequent gigs, I had been working with a bass player who seemed to take a sympathetic interest in my lonely plight. He collected me from my flat one weekend and drove me to a house in neighbouring Pimlico, promising to introduce me to a musician friend of his whose company he was sure I'd enjoy.

I took to Ron and his family immediately, as it seems they did to me. Although Ron and his wife were long established in England, I sensed a tinge

I Remember Me

of homesickness in them and the need for contact with a fellow Aussie, while I clung to the lifeline they threw to me with the desperate grasp of a drowning man. Ron provided me with vital inspiration and encouragement, his wife with a welcoming home to come to, and it was through their daughter Rel that I learnt to see London through different eyes. Rel was petite, with trusting eyes which lent her an appealing air of shyness. Yet from her finely sculptured, classical face there emanated a scholarly confidence. Well educated and highly intelligent, she was a credit to her generation and her good sense of fun made her exhilarating company. Ron very kindly allowed me the use of his Alvis panel-van to drive her as she guided me around her beloved city and showed me the sophistication of the metropolis. I realised just how much of a small town mentality I still had, as she opened my mind to the concept of vegetarianism, to classical music played by the famous orchestras in the big concert halls, and to the guitar genius of Segovia.

Meanwhile, it was now time to launch a renewed onslaught onto the record charts. Boosted by the success of *Lucky Devil*, I threw caution to the winds and went for another cover version of an American hit - this time the Paul Evans recording of *Happy Go Lucky Me*. There was nothing happy or lucky about it. George Formby covered it too, and since it was his first recording in many years, it was hardly surprising that his version gained maximum airplay, ruining my chances. If there was a lesson to be learned, it was not to jettison all my high ideals in such wild abandon.

Solace was to be found in a chance meeting with yet another Aussie ex-pat. As I continued to frequent Tin-Pan Alley, one of my regular ports of call was the publishing company, Southern Music. The manager, Bob Kingston, invited me to indulge myself to my heart's content in rummaging through their neglected country music catalogue. While I was elbow-deep in this pile of tapes, records and yellowing sheet music, I happened to ask Bob if he had any news of my old friend Allan Crawford who had been manager of the Australian branch of Southern Music back in 1952. It was to Allan I had spun that incredible yarn about a non-existent recording contract, just to persuade him to let me hear his new songs.

Bob surprised me by saying Allan was now stationed just across the way in Maddox Street with his own company, Merit Music. Well, I couldn't wait to see him after these many years, so with the same impetuosity I'd shown on that very first occasion, I rushed over to confront him there and then. Unlike our first encounter, this time I was welcomed like a long lost buddy. It was to be the first of many happy hours we would spend together, for we had an old friendship to renew, and much news to catch up on.

Allan was a man who was long on ideas but short on funds. I was short on funds too, but he soon had me inspired with the idea of forming my own music publishing company. As both publisher and performer, I was soon learning that openings for plugging songs and records were woefully few in Britain. With both of us coming from Australia, where radio opportunities abounded, we found this situation totally frustrating.

I had become somewhat disenchanted with British radio almost from the moment I set foot in Britain. With my resources stretched to the limit, there was frequently nothing left in the kitty to spare for entertainment, so most evenings were spent alone in my room listening to the radio. Yet, to hear pop music here, I had to tune either to Radio Luxembourg or to the American Forces Network and when the signal got too bad, I would resort to the BBC Light Programme, hoping to rediscover those wonderful radio shows I remembered from my early childhood. They proved to be few and far between and somehow it all seemed rather staid - a sorry substitute for the plethora of stations I was used to, where I was spoilt for choice in hearing my kind of music.

With my livelihood dependent on being able to sell my songs and records, the inadequacy of British radio had now become a matter of more than simple disillusionment. I opened up to Allan on the subject, lamenting the lack of independent radio, despairing at the restricted 'needle time' enforced by the Musician's Union on the BBC, and deploring Auntie BBC's own entrenched attitude of condescension towards pop music.

I was playing into the hands of a man with a mission.

"It's about time something was done to shake up Auntie's ideas then, isn't it?" he asked.

"Yes, but who's going to be able to do that?" I said.

"We can."

I stared at him. Was the man quite mad? "Oh yes - and just how are we two reprobates going to stand up against a national institution like the BBC?"

Allan had already planned precisely how it could be done. He had been waiting for the right person to confide in, someone who was impulsive and idealistic, someone with expertise gained from working in commercial radio, and someone with a vested interest in changing the status quo; in short, someone like me. He started to talk.

His hair-brained scheme sounded too far-fetched to be anything other than pie in the sky - a ship off the coast at Clacton bombarding the whole of south-east England with a broadside of jingles and pop tunes, it

I Remember Me

sounded more like Blackbeard in panto than a serious onslaught on the British airwaves - yet I found myself being drawn into the plot. I left him that night, my head buzzing with ideas, and when with the cold light of day, there still seemed to be a grain of possibility in the idea, I began to think maybe we had hit on something big.

But our 'something big' needed big money behind it. At this stage of the game, we were both miserably lacking in cash and it was far too risky a project to interest the big-time investors. For now, it would just have to stay under wraps.

♪ ♫ ♪ ♫ ♪

Meanwhile, my dogged persistence in haunting the offices of the music publishers of Tin Pan Alley was beginning to reap good dividends. I had already made the first of many appearances on Brian Matthews' BBC radio shows *Saturday Club* and *Easy Beat* and was now engaged as a regular on a lunchtime programme called *Parade Of the Pops* with Bob Miller & The Millermen, and compere Denny Piercy. Along with Vince Hill, Clinton Ford, Kathy Kirby and others, I was called upon to perform, live, a selection of the latest hits.

Once again, I was sacrificing my principles by readily agreeing to do something I had hitherto avoided at all costs - singing the hits of fellow artistes. But desperate times called for desperate measures. It was all very well having grandiose ideals when I had the security of living at home – but out here, I was on my own, fighting for survival.

Vince and I were nearly always chosen to sing the songs of artists with wide ranging voices and, invariably, I got the job of singing the Roy Orbison hits. Being a dedicated fan of the Big O, I admit this delighted me, but on a more pragmatic level, it was his songs especially that offered the opportunity to impress the powers-that-be with my own vocal ability. It's an ironic twist of fate that, later, Vince would be left to sing my hits on *Parade Of The Pops* - complete with falsetto.

This work was providing a regular income at last, and it also allowed Peter Gormley to start spreading his wings. He invested our meagre assets in the acquisition of the very chic address of 17 Saville Row, London, arguing that if you want to impress, you have got to be impressive.

Whether it was due to the address or not, the industry in general and Norrie Paramor in particular were evidently most impressed with Peter and his handling of my affairs. Norrie was A&R manager for Cliff Richard and the Shadows, and the members of the group had confided in

Norrie that they were looking to be represented separately from Cliff and were in the market for good management. Norrie suggested they approach Peter. Now, Peter and I had been a partnership ever since we teamed up in Australia back in 1958, so the decision to take them on had to be jointly made. The discussion didn't take long. This was an opportunity nobody of sane mind could refuse - so thus it came about that in June 1960 the Shadows joined our organisation.

Almost immediately afterwards, they shot to Number One with *Apache*. Peter and I were beside ourselves with glee. Our team had at last netted a winning goal. Even though it was not me who kicked the ball, I was overjoyed, as happy as if I had scored myself. That was all very well, but I couldn't afford to sit back and bask in the reflected glory of my new team-mates. I still needed a hit of my own.

I was pinning my hopes on my new release, *Gotta Get a Date*. It looked promising. Three disc jockey friends of mine - Barry Alldiss, Ted King and Ernie Williams - had a promotion running for this new record on Radio Luxembourg, and I was invited over to the Grand Duchy to join them. Ernie was a newcomer to Europe, but I had worked with him in Australia, where he is better known as TV and radio personality Ernie Siggley.

As part of the promotion, Radio Luxembourg organised a competition along the lines of 'What you would do if you had a date with Frank Ifield?' The competition prize was yours truly, and I was won by the pretty dark-eyed teenage daughter of the landlord of my new flat in Kensington. Sounds suspect? No, honestly, I had nothing to do with the outcome. She won legitimately by her own unselfish wish:

> *If I were to win a date with Frank Ifield, I would share the day with some underprivileged children and it would be a day out that they could always remember.*

That is just what happened. We took the children out for a wonderful boat-trip on the River Thames, which I have to admit to enjoying every bit as much as the kids did. As we slid past London's historic waterfront - the ancient Tower of London, with its notorious Traitor's Gate; Christopher Wren's spectacular dome of St Paul's; the Victorian magnificence of the Houses of Parliament with the world-famous Big Ben - I gained a new appreciation of just what a glorious city I was privileged to live in. Then to cap off a perfect day, we all went along to the fabulous London Palladium to see a show starring Cliff Richard.

I Remember Me

After the show, the big treat for the children was to go back stage with me to meet Cliff. Although he knew of me through my connections with Norrie Paramor and the Shadows, Cliff and I had never actually met before. However, the children assumed I must know him well and I didn't want to disillusion them. I fretted throughout the show, wondering how on earth I was going to avoid an embarrassment.

I needn't have worried. Cliff greeted me with the warmth of an old friend in just the way the kids expected. He spoke to all the children individually and I might easily have been equerry to the King himself in the admiring eyes of those kids on the way home. My prize-winner was right, it was indeed a day out we would always remember.

Cliff and the Shadows would later become great friends of mine. Here I am as a guest on Cliff's television show in 1963

As a result of everyone's efforts, the record entered the charts on September 29th 1960, roaring in from nowhere to number 49. Unfortunately, it roared straight out again, back to nowhere, taking me with it.

Not so the Shadows. Riding on the crest of their number one, they had become a hit attraction in their own right, and Peter had obtained a booking for them to star at the Globe Theatre in Stockton that winter. Since it was a Grades' Production, he'd also wangled a part for me in the same show - my very first pantomime. Although the undisputed stars were Bruce Welch, Hank B Marvin, Jet Harris and Tony Mehan, the original

Moss and Mayhem

members of The Shadows, I was honoured to find myself cast in the title role, Dick Whittington. Not having been brought up with the tradition of English pantomime, I had no idea what to expect. I thought of it as a kind of play with music, and I approached my role with some trepidation, regarding it as a serious portrayal of one of England's great folk heroes. I didn't see it in quite the same light when I discovered that my principal boy role was traditionally played by a girl dressed in tights.

I began to grasp the true nature of panto by watching the old troupers in rehearsal, people who had trodden the boards for a lifetime and exuded professionalism from their very fingertips. I soon realised the script was there to be taken liberties with, and I quickly fell into the pantomime custom of inserting something of myself. Yet I was dismayed, after our opening night, to read in the local paper that the reviewer had picked out for criticism my unscripted "Good on you cat".

Despite my unconventional characterisation, the show was a great success and the full house signs bore witness to that. I threw myself wholeheartedly into it, thankful to have something so absorbing to occupy my mind. Because whenever an idle moment came along, the cold of winter entered my heart and I'd be invaded with thoughts of home and family, thoughts that pricked my soul so painfully with yet another Christmas apart.

Desperately starved of affection, I offered no resistance when my empty heart surrendered to the spell of the bright-eyed, bubbly Iris. She was a dancer, a curly-haired blonde, whose tinkling laughter was simply intoxicating. Her nearness wrapped me in that secure warmth a cat feels when curled in front of the fire, and there was a lot to purr about when we were together.

Once I got into it, I found I loved pantomime, for I was allowed to do so much more than just sing. I could indulge the love of dressing-up and acting I had discovered as a child at school, draw upon my experience of playing comedy sketches in Australia and expand into the extra dimensions of romance and tragedy my role demanded. Pantomime also brought with it a whole new audience - the responsive, highly vocal and uninhibited enthusiasm of children. Absorbed in the drama, they watched wide-eyed with mouths agape, and it was a wonderful power I discovered, to be able to make them believe in me.

On one occasion, Cliff came to pay us a visit and, as a gag, we cajoled him into doing an impromptu walk-on, disguised as a pauper. Cliff, always ready for a bit of fun, was not difficult to persuade. We took him to wardrobe where they found a tattered cloak and hat, and when he

I Remember Me

saw himself dressed as a medieval mendicant, he laughed and said "Is this what my career has come down to?" Amazingly, he passed right across the stage, totally unrecognised by the audience. I wondered what their reaction would have been if he had raised his hat to reveal the famous face.

After a short run in Stockton, the production was dismantled then transported to a cinema in Hull where it was hurriedly re-erected. Because of the lack of overhead structures, all the pieces of hanging scenery had to be braced and converted to be free standing by placing weights at the bases. The makeshift modifications were far from ideal, but the show must go on.

'Overture and beginners' was called and the curtain rose to reveal the village scene with its painted houses. The dancers, dressed as villagers, were seen selling their wares in the opening sequence of *Who Will Buy?* and at the end of this song, the music gave my cue to make my first entrance. I sang...

Whenever I feel afraid, I hold my head erect...

As I walked across the stage, I had a vague impression of something moving towards me, but I ignored it.

I whistle a happy tune...

Suddenly - Whoosh! The back-flap whistled past my ears and crashed across the stage, crushing all beneath it... except me! Miraculously, I was left standing. I had passed right through the hole cut out for a window. Totally 'unflappable', I continued...

So no one will suspect I'm afraid...

Oh no! Out of the corner of my eye, I saw the prompt-side flap lurch in my direction. I braced myself. The audience gasped... and wallop! The scenery whacked down on top of me, only this time I ripped through it, cardboard and wood shattering all around me. Unsteady but unscathed, I carried on...

While shivering in my shoes...

The last remaining flap was now hovering dangerously. Pandemonium erupted in the audience as inevitably it, too, piled down onto the stage. It missed me but on its way it demolished a 'tree' that was left to teeter on the edge of the orchestra pit, menacing the brass section, who stopped playing. I persisted doggedly in fighting on to the end of the song, though the music petered out, and the uproar in the auditorium drowned my voice. Desperately, I looked for Idle Jack to appear as he should have done, but no one came to my rescue. Instead, I stood out there alone, knee deep in debris, for what seemed an eternity while a bewildered crew rushed about in confusion behind me, and excited children out front screamed with laughter.

Finally, we attempted to restart from the entrance of Idle Jack. However, when I turned to deliver my dialogue, I was confronted instead by Dopey, the dwarf from Snow White, his trouser legs dragging on the floor beneath his feet and his jacket swamping his diminutive frame.

Unbeknown to me, there had been ructions in the wings. Ken Platt, the popular North Country comedian who was playing Idle Jack, declared the whole thing too dangerous and refused to go on. So, undaunted, Charles King, our producer, scriptwriter and company manager, had taken over his role. Whereas Ken was a tall strapping fellow, Charles was the other extreme.

How I managed to stop myself corpsing on the spot I'll never know - but it was all too much for Charles. Just when I thought things couldn't possibly get worse, he blew a mental fuse right there in front of me and completely forgot his lines. Although I tried to prompt him, Charles was beyond help, so I had to continue as best I could, speaking his dialogue as well as my own.

Eventually, the panto got back into full swing, but how we ever got through it remains a mystery. The audience had a whale of a time, enjoying every calamity to the full, but for us, especially me, it was the sort of horror of which nightmares are made.

When the last curtain fell and the time came to part from the cast, I was inexplicably sad, knowing I would miss the companionship I had found with the company. They'd become like a family to me, dispelling for a short while the feeling of loneliness that had haunted me since I'd left home. Most of all I would miss Iris. To be separated from her was going to leave an even emptier place in my heart and I vowed to her I would see her again. But in the itinerant wanderings of a showbiz life, such promises are easily made but not so easily kept. Somehow we lost each other in the mists of time.

♪♫♪♫♪

I Remember Me

Before long I was on the road again. Reunited with Kathy Kirby and Alan Randall, I was this time supporting, with them, American superstar guitarist Duane Eddy on his April 1961 tour. The tour was such a resounding success that it was booked into the Finsbury Park Empire for an extra week. I was thankful to Duane Eddy's manager, Lee Hazelwood, for requesting me for this unscheduled week, because it was not only my first London West End show, it was heaven-sent opportunity to prove myself to the revered Moss Empire circuit.

There were few variety theatres still functioning around the country, and of the ones remaining, the most flourishing was the Moss Empire circuit. However, competition was fierce and it was difficult to achieve a contract. I made it my business to discover just how best to impress the Moss Empire booker Cissy Williams.

"Wear blue - you'll have a better chance" was the whisper put about by the show's up-and-coming comic, Des O'Connor. I went out and bought blue.

I was to start my spot with the dynamic Marv Johnson hit *You Got What It Takes*. We'd paid meticulous attention to this number at rehearsal to get the tempo and feel just right, so it was with great confidence I waited to begin. But I couldn't believe my ears when the conductor, Sid Caplan, counted it in. It was played so fast and so badly it was all I could do to keep up. My act was being sabotaged and my high hopes were plummeting.

I noticed, though, that Kathy Kirby's music was played superbly well. I asked her manager, Ambrose, how she had achieved it.

"Buy a set of music covers from Sid Caplan - your music will be played to perfection."

It went against my principles but I placed an order for them and my musical score was spot-on for the second show.

As a consequence of the enthusiastic audience reaction to my performance - or maybe it was the blue suit? - Cissy Williams approved and I passed the criteria for touring the Moss Empire circuit.

So the bookings for the top Empire theatres began to roll in and I was getting the stage experience I had hungered for, but it was all support work. Ten to fifteen minutes on the variety stage offered little chance to extend and develop my act. Then one day an offer came in from the Royalty Theatre in Chester to headline for a week. It didn't mean I'd hit the big time, for the Royalty was only a small provincial theatre, but nonetheless it was a terrific opportunity for me to show the world what I could do, and I jumped at it.

It was obvious that the band did not view the occasion with the same importance as I did, for when I arrived for rehearsal, half of them had not bothered to turn up. I was livid. I wasn't being paid enough to employ Liverpool musicians at the eleventh hour, so I was forced to dismiss what remained of the band, abandon my carefully prepared programme and take up my guitar.

Pretty soon, though, I was enjoying my unfettered impromptu performance, sliding comfortably back into the role of singer-guitarist I had left behind on Australia's shore. Carried along on a wave of nostalgia, I launched happily into all those songs I had only ever performed back home, music that belonged to a Frank Ifield the British public had not been aware of. The half-empty theatre filled with loud applause as the audience lapped it up.

Then came the inevitable moment when I just had to produce the yodel. Nothing half-hearted, this crowd deserved the best, the real thing, and I gave it to them - a full-throated rendition of *She Taught Me How To Yodel*. Whether it was surprise, shock, or sheer amazement, the audience went wild. I was ecstatic. The show could have been total disaster, but I'd managed to turn it into a triumph.

I could see Peter Gormley in the wings, tutting and shaking his head, and I hardly dared leave the stage, sure I was in for trouble. I'd broken all the rules Peter had imposed on me when we'd left Australia - especially his strict ban on the yodel.

From the outset, Peter had warned me that because yodelling was unusual in England, it would be seen as a gimmick - and once the public cottons onto a novelty, then it is by this they will always know you. Any other ability you might have will become shrouded in its shadow, which, in aiming for acceptance as an all-round performer, was something I certainly did not want to happen.

But I'd done it now. I'd let the yodel out of the bag - and Peter was right. The news spread like a raging bush-fire and my fame grew so much during the week, that on my return to the nearby Liverpool Empire as support act to The Shadows, people travelled over from Chester specifically in the hope of a repeat performance. They should have been sadly disappointed. However, they called for it over and over again, so I had no choice - in order to obey the wishes of my growing following of fans, I was compelled to continue disobeying Peter.

♪♫♪♫♪

I Remember Me

While I'd been plodding my way uphill, Peter had set a cracking pace with the acquisition of the Shadows. Then, in March 1961, Cliff Richard himself sought new management. Naturally he was acquainted with Peter's competent handling of the Shadows, so it was to us he turned. As for Peter and me, there was no decision to make - we welcomed him into our establishment with open arms.

Mind you, it was a different ball game now Peter had Cliff as well as the Shadows as his front line giants, and I began to worry I would be relegated to a mere reserve, sitting on the sidelines. Would Peter still be interested in calling my shots, or did this mean the end of the game for me?

- 15 -
STILL CHASING RAINBOWS

"You should keep it in your act Frank, it's good for a laugh."

Rushing out to reach the waiting audience, I'd caught my heel on the edge of the raised platform and - splat! - I'd sprawled full-length, with my nose flattened firmly against a face-full of stage. It was the opening night of my very first summer season, and I'd so wanted to make an impression, but not with my chin.

The voice that greeted me, when my red face and I thankfully left the stage, was that of Bernie Winters. He was starring in the show, at Swanson's Cabaret, St Helier in Jersey, with his brother Mike, the other half of the famous comedy duo.

Needless to say, I wasn't keen to follow his advice. However, Bernie obviously considered I was in need of further guidance, for he took me under his wing as both friend and tutor. One day he said to me "You're a good singer Frank, your choice of songs is fine, but you need to present yourself BIG to the audience."

I was taken aback by this. It was exactly what I had striven to do in all my years of performing.

"How do you mean?"

"You've got to make everything larger than life. Think of your presentation. Your shoes mustn't just shine they must GLISTEN. Your stage suits must be immaculately tailored and ULTRA smart."

"I'm doing my level best, Bernie, but it's difficult. Work's been a bit thin since I came to England and I really can't afford to buy anything better."

He replied by saying something I shall remember ever more.

"You can't afford NOT to. You must HAVE the best if you want to BE the best. To become a star, first LOOK like a star."

Another day, it was my musical arrangements that came under scrutiny. There was no way I could afford to pay a copyist, so I had been doing the copying of my own musical scores.

But Bernie insisted it was just not good enough. He advised me to go and talk to a guy called Johnny Hawkins, who was playing saxophone and piano in a band show nearby. Johnny came to see my act and afterwards said that, yes, he'd like to work with me and offered to let me pay "sometime later".

I accepted.

I Remember Me

With Johnny Hawkins (soon nicknamed 'The Hawk'), I worked long and hard at injecting style and sparkle into my arrangements, so whenever I felt I'd earned a break, I'd head to the beach at St Owens to relax in the company of the rest of the cast. One day, I got more of a break than I'd bargained for when I broke my toe playing football barefoot on the sand. I was still nursing the damaged digit when, on the 29th May, Mum, Dad, my brother John and his new bride Jan all arrived in London.

All through the long year and a half since I arrived in Britain, Mum's letters to me had been as manna in the wilderness. I watched the mail each day for an airmail letter in her handwriting, and as soon as I got it, I'd tear open the flap and digest all the news of home. One letter especially had bitten deep at my very heartstrings, when I read of my brother John's marriage to Jan at the little old church of St Jude in my childhood home, Dural. John was the first of my brothers to wed. I could visualise them all gathering outside the church: the bride and groom, Mum, Dad, Gran, my brothers, aunts and uncles, cousins, dear friends and neighbours - in fact everybody except me. My isolation had hit me very hard right then.

And now, wouldn't you know it? After weeks of no work, with free time hanging heavy on my hands, they came to visit England when my working life was suddenly full. I was mortified not to be at the airport to greet them myself, but Peter met them on my behalf, while I had to make do with the sound of their voices over the telephone wires. Until Sunday, that was, when early in the morning mist, I flew across to Birmingham to be with them.

I saw very little of John, as he and Jan were hell bent on doing their own thing on their belated honeymoon. However, there was never a lull in conversation with Mum and Dad as I caught up on all the gossip from home. On Monday afternoon, Mum accompanied me back to Jersey for few days, and I attempted to fill in all the missing pieces of the jigsaw puzzle that was my life, while we savoured the delights of the beautiful sunny island and its famous cream teas. Jersey is a wonderful mixture of the lush green beauty of England and the sandy beaches of Sydney, and its people are the friendliest folk you could ever hope to meet. Mum and I enjoyed their hospitality and our precious time together immensely, but Thursday came around too soon and at 4pm, we found ourselves back at Jersey airport where I sadly waved her off to rejoin Dad in Birmingham.

To quell the renewed pangs of homesickness, I attempted to conjure Australia by laying in the sun on the warm Jersey sand, closing my eyes and letting the sound of the surf drift me homeward. As it happened, though, my spirits were lifted, not by the bright summer weather, but by the sunshine of a summer romance.

She was a showgirl and her name was Lynne. She was leggy, lithe and lovely and endowed with the figure of a golden goddess. Her essence surrounded my being and, overwhelmed by the need to have someone near who cared, my heart cried of love and I believed it. She responded to my timorous approaches with a warmth that lit fires deep within me. I was besotted by the beauty of this blue eyed blonde and could not get her out of my mind.

I can only blame the wine and the full moon for what happened next. Lured by the romantic light of the moon, we bathed together at midnight in the silver sea. Bursting with emotion, I took her hand and to the soft swish and sway of waves washing on the shore, I asked her if we could become engaged. Her eyes twinkled in tune with the stars as she smiled her emphatic "yes".

That weekend, we attended a party graced by many showbiz celebrities. Proudly, she showed off her brand new ring while I preened myself as the object of everyone's congratulations. That is, I did until band singer Vera Day took me aside to offer her own good wishes on our engagement, and asked the crucial question "When will the wedding be?"

Wedding? I staggered under the enormity of it. It sounded so final - yet I'd only known Lynne for a week. To me, the ring represented a statement that we were going steady, nothing more - I wasn't ready to lose my independence and I certainly wasn't ready to be married. Yet, after one look at the happy smile on the face of the girl who wore the ring, I knew I couldn't tell her I was having second thoughts.

By the end of the season, I was still unsure, yet as it would mean losing her, I found I simply could not break off the engagement. My show finished before hers, so I went to London in search of an apartment for us. I returned to Jersey only to be given the whisper by a friend that while I had been gone, Lynne had been seeing her former boyfriend. I confronted her and she admitted it was true. My ego was deflated, but my escape was secured. As for the engagement ring, that probably lays even now under a bramble bush in a Jersey hedgerow.

♪♫♪♫♪

While the summer in Jersey may have left my emotions drained, it had topped up my finances, putting me in the joyful state of being able to afford something a little better than my previous abodes.

During a *Saturday Club* for BBC Radio, I happened to mention to Ian Grant, producer of the show, that I was flat-hunting. Ian told me there was a

I Remember Me

flat going in the block where he lived, and that evening he took me along to see Charlie Bourke, manager of Cleveland Mansions, Paddington. Charlie showed me apartment 5 and I took it on the spot.

The establishment was a glorified theatrical digs, and I settled in very easily, soon feeling at home here in the company of a bunch of hopefuls just like myself. We would congregate together in the communal bar, where there was always someone strumming a guitar, writing a song, working out new material, or just singing for the sheer hell of it.

Rehearsing with the Viscounts

I already knew some of the residents, such as Gerry Dorsey, who lived next door to me in number 6 and whom I'd met in Jersey, and Gordon Mills who was a member of the Viscounts, a group I'd worked with on many occasions. My other next-door neighbour, in number 4, was one of Larry Parnes's protégés, to whom he had given the wondrous name of Duffy Power. Larry was a successful showbusiness manager and impresario, who delighted in giving his artists forceful names such as Marty Wilde, Billy Fury, Vince Eager and Johnny Gentle.

Gordon suggested that a new name might well improve my chances. Peter and I did at one time consider a stage name for me because Americans found it hard to pronounce my surname, but we hadn't come up with a suitable alternative. However, Gordon and I spent an hilarious evening laughing over the ridiculous names we invented for me - Freddy Flange and Frank the Wank being two that spring to mind. Needless to say, I didn't take

Still Chasing Rainbows

seriously any of Gordon's wild suggestions, but my neighbour Gerry would eventually do so. A couple of years later Gordon became his manager and allotted him one of the most contrived names of all - Engelbert Humperdinck.

♪♫♪♫♪

I needn't have worried that Peter would lose interest in me once he had Cliff and the Shadows. Peter was a gentleman and would never go back on his word. In fact, there were now six heads working hard to find a winning formula for me and with talent like that fighting on my side, I felt I surely must break through soon. So when Bruce Welch and Hank Marvin came up with a song specially written for my next release, I was convinced I was at last on my way to a major hit. It was released before my Jersey season, but instead of storming forth like a lion, *That's The Way It Goes* crept out like a mouse - and that's the way it went, taking my eagerly anticipated hit with it.

For the follow-up, I wanted to use a song I had already been performing as a production number in my act while on tour with the Shadows. It was *Tobacco Road*, one of those old country songs I had unearthed in the archives of Southern Music. I'd given it a forceful, dramatic treatment that always received a great reaction, and was convinced that with this proven appeal it ought to do well. Norrie Paramor agreed I should record the song, but then consigned it to the flip side of an inconsequential, sing-along ditty called *Life's a Holiday*, which consequentially became a huge flop. *Tobacco Road*, on the other hand, did eventually reach the Top Ten in 1964 - recorded by the Nashville Teens.

By the end of 1961, I'd been in England for two years and I was still chasing rainbows. In the early days I could tell myself I needed time, I couldn't expect to hit the jackpot straight away. But now that excuse was wearing thin. However, it's not in my nature to surrender before I have battled to the bitter end, so the struggle to find the 'biggie' went on.

I wasn't short of allies in my battle, and the next to come to my aid was Vince Hill who wrote for me a song called *Alone Too Long*, which became my next single. In an attempt to acquire as much peak exposure as possible, EMI submitted the song as a contender for the United Kingdom's entry for the 1962 Eurovision Song Contest.

This was not the first big song contest in which I had chanced my luck. Back in March of 1961, I had entered Associated Rediffusion's British TV Song Contest with a strong original song called *I Can't Get Enough Of Your Kisses*. Here, I vied with my friend and fellow Sagittarian Matt Monro, whose song was *My Kind Of Girl*. True to our gambling sign, we took bets on which

I Remember Me

of us would win, but as it turned out, neither of us did. The contest was won by Michael Cox with his entry *In The Springtime*, which thereafter descended into total oblivion. Based on this, and the fact I came only third, it was decided not to issue my entry as a single. Matt, who had come second, did release his and went on to gain an enormous big hit with *My Kind Of Girl* which, of course, became one of his most famous songs. Meanwhile, and out of sheer spite it would seem, my song leapt up to number one in the sheet music charts, whilst I was left to gnash my teeth at such a wasted opportunity.

Determined not to waste this one, I performed *Alone Too Long* in front of a huge audience in BBC TV's *Song for Europe* and prayed desperately for the win which would take me on to the big Europe-wide televised contest and the enormous publicity it would bring in its wake. In the event, the song gained a lot of votes but I won only a little credibility and a lot more frustration, coming in second to Ronnie Carroll's *Ring-A-Ding Girl*. The 'biggie' was just as elusive as ever.

Time was now running desperately short. There was only one more single to be released on my two year contract with EMI, and everything depended on this one, for if it failed to make a big impact, the contract might not be renewed and that would be the end of my chances. Yet what could I try next? As far as I could see, there was only one avenue left. It was time to reinstate that philosophy which had stood me in such good stead back in Australia: to trust in my intuition and my own individuality.

To this end, I had been working in secret on a novel concept that had long been buzzing around my brain – to take a standard song and give it a laid back country feel. I'd found many songs fitted comfortably into this format. Even with those which didn't, it was a simple matter of taking a few liberties - changing the beat to bring it more up-to-date, simplifying the chord structures, modifying the tune slightly to fit, altering a few words here and there and, as a final flourish, adding a falsetto inflection to brand it with my identity. I was confident that at last I had found what I'd long been seeking - an original presentation that was uniquely my own.

I had a couple of songs prepared in this new style and was ready to stake my future on it. All that remained was to convince Norrie Paramor.

- 16 -

MAKE WITH THE EYES AND TEETH

I swept into Norrie's office, guitar at the ready, and with my usual fiery exuberance, I set about singing. For my first song I chose *Confessin'*, a well-known standard fitting perfectly into my brand new format. All the time I was performing, I was searching his face for a glimmer of acceptance. It didn't appear. At the conclusion, he nodded, raised one eyebrow, and through pursed lips mumbled "Hmm."

"Not bad, eh?" I confirmed on his behalf. "Just wait till you hear my second song."

This one was a little more complicated, requiring almost a rewrite. It was written back in 1942 for Paramount Picture's unmemorable wartime musical movie, *The Fleets In*, starring Dorothy Lamour and William Holden. Apart from its stars, the film's saving grace was that it featured some great tunes from the prolific pen of Johnny Mercer. Melodies such as the title song *The Fleets In* and *Tangerine* were very popular at the time but the one I had chosen was lesser known.

> *... When my life is through*
> *and the angels ask me to recall*
> *the thrill of them all*
> *then I will tell them*
> *I remember you.*

As I reached the falsetto crescendo and the final chord died away, I looked up eagerly for the anticipated favourable reaction from Norrie. It was not forthcoming. Without comment, he politely excused himself, rose from his chair and left the room.

That was it then, was it? After all those long hours spent in solitary toil? I could hardly credit that he seemed so lukewarm over my new concept and I tried to find reasons for his apparent lack of enthusiasm. Maybe it was because the songs were well known to him – after all, he would have often played them during his jazz days touring with Harry Gold's band Pieces Of Eight. Or perhaps *I Remember You* was a favourite of his and he didn't appreciate the fact that I'd changed it so much, or was it that the falsetto was just too much of a shock for him to take? I'd not dared use it in front of Norrie before because Peter Gormley was so adamant I should not.

I Remember Me

If I couldn't persuade Norrie of its potential then my hopes were doomed and all my hard work in vain. I slumped into the chair, sinking deeper into despondency, while in the deathly quiet of the room I could hear my pulse building up pressure.

The frosted-glass door between the outer office and me was slightly ajar and I could hear conversation. While I'd been singing, Peter had arrived and he and Norrie were now talking together out there. Suddenly, breaking into my melancholy, came Peter's voice desperately trying to convince Norrie to play ball.

"Go ahead and record it - what have you got to lose? It's the last record on his contract anyhow."

Indeed, Peter had his own axe to grind. *I Remember You* had originally been his suggestion two years ago, but it had taken me this length of time to find what I considered was the right treatment for it.

They entered the room. Bravely, I raised a half smile and offered a murmur of greeting to Peter that was all but ignored. However, Norrie seemed moved by the unprecedented sight of my glum face.

"Let me hear them again," he said. "Sing the songs and I'll put them on tape and think about them later."

When this was accomplished they changed the topic to discussing Cliff Richard's next release and I took my leave.

Even the underground train had found its own rhythm, I thought, as it rattled on its way to my stop - so why couldn't I? This time I had honestly believed I was on the right track. Morbid thoughts of making this my final curtain call came to my mind, but I banished them quickly.

"Oh well," I sighed, "I'll have to take it from the top and find a brand new tactic - but what?"

I fumbled for the key to open the front door of the hollow-ringing place called home and dragged myself up the stairs. I put my guitar down quickly before it tempted me to play the blues and waited instead for the bubbly singing of the kettle to cheer me up, although my brain was far too numbed by self-doubt to gain an uplift from a mere dose of caffeine. No, what was needed was a flash of musical inspiration, yet there was none. The empty passing of time was measured only by the draining of the coffee pot.

The doorbell shattered the silence. Slowly, I descended the gloomy staircase, hoping it was no one for whom I would need to fix on a cheerful face. It was Peter. This unexpected visit could only mean one thing and I stood transfixed, expecting to hear the worst. He played dumb for the agonising length of time it took us to climb the stairs, then...

Make With the Eyes and Teeth

"Norrie's confirmed a recording date. He's going to record *I Remember You*"

I turned a smile at him that could have lit up the universe. He told me that after listening to the tape over and over again, Norrie had begun to feel quietly enthusiastic about it and wanted to do the musical score himself. In my relief, I didn't know whether to laugh or cry, so I picked up my guitar, cradled her in my arms and danced round and around the room.

Norrie phoned a few days later to ask me to his house in Bishops Avenue. The invitation was not unusual. Norrie liked to treat his artists as friends, and I was always delighted to visit his home, where he and his lovely wife Joan always made me feel one of the family. This time, the invitation was more to do with business than pleasure, but even so I certainly felt more at ease with Norrie here than in his office. Sitting back in an easy chair, he explained the reason for his initial reaction to my treatment of the song.

"It was so unique," he said, "it took me completely by surprise. But now I've had time to think..." His face mellowed to a grin as he leant towards me. "Frank, we've been a long while searching for your individualism and I think we might finally have found it in your yodel." Then the smile died and a perplexed, almost pained expression took its place. "But what I don't understand is - why have you kept it hidden from me all this time?"

"Peter didn't want me to use it," I said sheepishly.

I really couldn't do right for doing wrong here, could I? On the one hand I risked angering Peter because I had revealed my yodel and on the other Norrie was now upset because I had not. However, it was only a smidgen of falsetto, hardly a fully-fledged yodel, and hopefully I could keep them both happy by going no further than that.

With the rift healed, Norrie and I relaxed into our usual rapport and got down together to work on the arrangement. Norrie had decided to mix classical strings with the pop/country feel I had given this standard jazz song and hoped the differing styles would blend amicably. However, I wasn't altogether happy with the idea. Excited by the raw vibrancy of the music on some of the latest hits, notably Bruce Channel's *Hey Baby*, I was keen to capture that 'back to basics' freshness to complement the simplicity of my new styling. A full string arrangement would sound too polished.

"I don't think we should use violins," I said.

I was risking my neck here - Norrie was one of the best string arrangers around. I admit to being surprised when he agreed with me.

I Remember Me

"OK. What would you suggest?" he asked.

"Four cellos," I said. "Cellos would lay a rich foundation to the rhythm section and they'd be felt rather than actually heard."

Norrie seemed startled. "Do you realise that a cello quartet hasn't been used before in a pop song?"

Nevertheless, a thoughtful expression was stealing all over his face.

♪♫♪♫♪

The 27th May was the date set for the recording session. I had done many sessions at Abbey Road studios, so what made this one so special? I reckon it was a combination of things: the fact that Norrie had usually been with me in the capacity of record producer, overseeing the session from the control room, whereas this time he was my arranger and conductor; also this was the first time I was to record this new-found original style and was anxious about how it would turn out; and then there was the uncertainty of the orchestral combination.

True to my custom, I was there an hour or so early, just to soak up the ambience and to re-acquaint myself with my surroundings. The staff were already preparing the studio by setting up the microphones, music stands and my acoustic screens. These were even now being repositioned for me to see Malcolm Addey, EMI's chief recording technician, in the recording booth, while at the same time enabling me to feel a part of the band and able to watch Norrie for directions. I kicked off my shoes, as I always did. It's a throwback to my childhood days in the Australian bush - I always feel more comfortable barefoot.

Musicians began straggling in. First came two men sharing a joke as they opened their guitar cases. Then, the double bass player came in and while I was greeting them, the drummer appeared, seated himself behind the kit and began toying with the cymbals and practising with his brushes. Over on the other side of the studio, a man, whose name was Harry Pitch, had opened his bag on a chair and was taking out several mouth organs, blowing a test on each one.

One of the staff returned to place the music on the appropriate stands, and as he left, four more figures entered the room. Dressed formally in shirts and ties, they had the appearance of being ready for the concert platform rather than a recording studio. Self-consciously, they huddled together in a quartet and I watched with a deepening glow of satisfaction as they carefully unpacked their cellos.

Make With the Eyes and Teeth

Until now, I'd managed to remain calm, but as each musician tuned and warmed up, an excitement began to well up inside me. Norrie appeared with his portfolio of musical scores tucked under his arm and a brief hush descended on the studio while the maestro's entrance received the due reverence reserved for one of nature's true gentlemen. After he'd wished us all good afternoon, I turned back to the guitarist, to whom I was attempting to demonstrate the open-chord rhythm-sound I wanted. I'd been showing him on my round-hole acoustic Gibson J200, which sounded better than his basic flat-top model. Just as I was handing him my guitar to use on the session, I was suddenly aware of Norrie glaring at me over the top of his glasses.

Norrie Paramor, A&R manager for EMI's Columbia label. My friend and mentor, and the man behind all my big hit records.

"Frank, all you have to do is sing the song."

Yes, he put me firmly in my place. He was absolutely right, of course, yet throughout my recording career, I have needed to take control, not feeling able to rely upon anyone else to reproduce my ideas. Brought to heel, I stood like a naughty schoolboy alongside Norrie's raised dais, listening while the band struck up for a preliminary check of the arrangement.

This nine-piece band might have been one of the smallest Norrie had conducted, but nevertheless he'd written a sympathetic arrangement that unfolded like a dream, flowing so sweetly and following so closely to my simplified guitar chord structure.

I sang quietly to myself, rehearsing my own performance while they played. Norrie must have sensed I was in need of some reassurance from him, for he leaned over and confided:

"I feel a real buzz about this one, Frank. I'm convinced we're onto something big."

I Remember Me

I sensed a glow of pride and relief at these words after all I'd been through to persuade him.

Now it was my turn. With a rat-a-tat of his baton on the music stand, Norrie signalled the band to order. He beckoned me to sing, winking at me through his glasses as he quipped "Now Frank, make with the eyes and teeth."

I knew straightaway what he meant. You see, according to Norrie, my secret ingredient was that I projected my voice better when I was smiling and so we always liked to keep an air of good humour when doing our sessions. Yes, he'd put me at ease, made me smile and now I was in the mood to sing.

The intro started with the simple strumming guitar followed by the raw sound of Harry Pitch on mouth-harp. After he had played the first five notes, the rich, sophisticated sound of the cellos took up, causing a shiver to run down my spine. This was it. I cupped my hand to my ear and performed the song as easily as if I was rehearsing it in my bathroom at home.

We were ready for the first take. I entered my little baffle-box and sang my heart out. I prepared myself for a second run, but...

"I think that's a take," I heard from the control room. "What's next?"

"Hopefully, a number one!" I replied, hearing my own voice echo the sentiment back from the now open door of the control room.

Norrie and I went together into the booth to listen to the playback. You can have a gut feeling about a project but it's only when you get to this stage you realise what you have got.

"What you hear there is the jingling sound of the cash register," pronounced Norrie.

"That mouth-harp phrase was indeed a stroke of genius," I said. "It's added that hook, that touch of sheer magic."

"Do you recognise the phrase?" asked Norrie, scratching an itch beneath his hairpiece with his baton.

I turned to him and could see my own vacuous expression reflected in his glasses, as he elucidated:

"It's the first five notes of the chorus of *Waltzing Matilda*."

That was typical of Norrie's tongue-in-cheekiness, I thought.

♪♫♪♫♪

I had squeezed this recording session in whilst touring with American singing star Bruce Channel, following his springtime No. 2 hit, *Hey Baby*.

He was top of the bill, with big name support acts Johnny Kidd and the Pirates, Cliff Bennett and the Rebel Rousers and compere Diz Disley, while I was still just one of the 'wines and spirits'. However there were perks even for the likes of me. For some reason, teenage girls seem to be attracted to showbiz like moths to a flame, which gives an added meaning to the phrase 'one-night stand'. Most of these sexual encounters are but fleeting - instantly gratifying, rarely lasting. Yet somehow I knew at once that this one was going to be different.

I was at the stage door at the Colston Hall, Bristol, fighting my way through the milling crowd, when suddenly I found myself gazing upon a face softly radiating its welcome like a beacon in a storm. Her dark brown eyes looked up to me with the open appeal of a puppy and her dimpled cheeks broke into a grin so infectious, I couldn't help but return it. Her hand brushed against mine as I moved forward and a spark of instant chemistry flashed between us.

Margaret materialised at a time of great expectation in my life - a time also fraught with suspense while I awaited the record release. She accompanied me through the remainder of my tour with Bruce Channel, offering her loving trust and wide-eyed wonder. In her, I found a release from the intolerable pressure I was under.

Listening to Bruce live in the theatre, I was even more impressed by the excitement and immediacy of his music, and convinced I had taken the right approach with the arrangement of *I Remember You* – right down to that distinctive harmonica phrase. I had not dared to sing *I Remember You* on tour for fear of it being plagiarised and recorded by someone else before I had chance to get it out. After all, it could have been a perfect vehicle for Bruce himself, his harmonica player Delbert McClinton who was a well-known Country singer, or even the talented members of our backing band, including Frank Allen on bass, who soon after became a founder member of the Searchers.

However, I was eager to see what reaction it would receive from a live audience. I judged the time was ripe when I was booked for a week's cabaret at the newly opened Webbington Country Club near Margaret's home town of Bristol.

The first show was early in the week and it wasn't a full house. Although the audience responded warmly to me, they were somewhat subdued - until I sang *I Remember You*. Suddenly, they went mad. You'd have thought the room was filled twice over as they called for me to repeat it time and time again.

I Remember Me

At last, I had some proof the song did indeed have public appeal. Furthermore, the word spread like whispers on the wind and the very next night the place was packed. The atmosphere was electric - I could feel the expectancy in the audience even before I made my appearance. Night after night, the capacity crowds grew more and more wild in their enthusiasm, so that by the end of the week I was certain I was onto a real humdinger. The tension had been unbearable and now the relief was sheer exhilaration, and it was a joy to share it with my lovely companion, Dolly, as I had come to call her. The manager, for his part, was so delighted with the custom I had attracted to his new establishment that he offered us free room and board for the week.

♪♫♪♫♪

The record was beginning to attract attention in other quarters too. I was both surprised and delighted when I received a cable from Cliff who was filming *Summer Holiday* in Athens at the time. He had listened to an early pressing and was moved to express this comment: "This is not only the best record you've ever made, it's one of the greatest records ever."

Praise indeed from one who has proved beyond doubt that he possesses the magic touch.

The BBC and Radio Luxembourg, were now starting to give the record high rotation. Then, to coincide with its release, it was featured on BBC TV's *Jukebox Jury* and unanimously voted a resounding hit. Unfortunately, I didn't see the show as I was working, but the result was relayed to me eagerly by everyone I met. However, I didn't dare believe it could make the charts until I read it for myself in a newspaper. Can you imagine the thrill? There was the proof in print that on July 5th 1962, just one week after its release, my record had entered the Top Thirty.

♪♫♪♫♪

It was the morning of 18th July and I was back in London. It was a beautiful day and the warm sunshine outside my window dispelled the dreariness of my little flat. The phone rang. No sooner had I picked it up than an impassioned voice cried out at me down the line:

"You've done it!"

It was Peter Gormley - or at least I thought it was, because he was hardly recognisable. It was almost unknown for him to be roused to such a level of excitement.

Make With the Eyes and Teeth

"You're Number One, Frank! Congratulations!"

"What? Are you sure?"

I was as ecstatic as a dog with two tails. Overwhelmed, I couldn't keep from doing knee bends on the spot. Even before the enormity of the event had time to sink in, the phone rang again. This time it was Norrie adding to my euphoria by telling me that on this day alone, I'd sold an incredible 102,500 records.

Suddenly, the world was on my phone making it nigh impossible for me to reserve a call to my home in Australia. Finally, I managed it.

I began to get a knotted feeling in the pit of my stomach as I listened to that familiar ringing tone. I could visualise the phone sitting on the hall table, its strident bell sounding throughout our house, and I waited impatiently for whoever would answer.

"Hello - yes," came my mother's warm and dulcet tones that immediately cut the intervening miles down to size.

"Hello Mum. It's me - Frank - I'm phoning from England." I could hear my own voice echo my excitement as I continued, "I've got some wonderful news for you all."

"Hello dear, just a minute 'til I call the family... Boys! Come quick, it's Frank on the line from England..."

Once Mum had returned to listening mode, I explained I was Number One in the British Hit Parade.

"Oh? That's nice dear - congratulations - we've been expecting it. Even though it isn't released here yet, John Laws and one or two other deejays have just started to play it."

Our John's voice interjected, "Hey Frank! That's great news!"

Then bedlam reigned on the other end of the line as each of my brothers, Mum, Dad and Gran all tried to speak at once. I could hear tears and lumps of pride stick in their throats as they sent joy and happiness for me across the twelve thousand miles. They even put my dog Rover on the phone - he evidently cocked an ear and leaned his head to one side to hear his master's voice, but was obviously struck dumb by the news.

I really couldn't say a lot more, other than "I wish you were all here. I love you all and miss you madly."

The call concluded with Dad taking over, saying "Frank, we're all so proud of you son, especially me. Now, don't get carried away or let success change you. Remember, you will always be our Frank, no matter what life holds in store for you."

Finally, to the clutter of cheerios, I choked my "goodbye" and tears welled up in my eyes as I replaced the receiver. Even in the dizzy heights

I Remember Me

of my euphoria, I could feel the waves of longing for my family washing over me.

Thank goodness I had Dolly to turn to. She wore her happy face and dressed herself in a radiance that matched my own. Joined by friends, we went out together that night to celebrate in champagne style by going to see Shirley Bassey at London's fashionable theatre night-club, The Talk Of The Town.

♪♫♪♫♪

If the pundits were right, and all I needed was a big hit, then now, surely, it would all begin to take off? Well, they were right and it did - I was away off the blocks like a runner with a rocket behind me. Instead of anxiously seeking bookings, I was now inundated with them. The Grade Organisation swung into action as promised and suddenly I was everywhere - in the press, on the radio and all over the TV screens. For a purely personal reason, I was overjoyed with the TV show that was chosen to be the first.

Right from my early days in England, I was lucky to have found a champion in that wonderfully talented singer, Alma Cogan, who had no less than 20 hits to her own credit. Convinced one day I would find success, she had clung fervently to her belief, all the while encouraging and spurring me on to do better. At this time, she was the regular host of Associated Rediffussion's Saturday night TV spectacular and it seemed so fitting it was she who would present the first TV airing of my *I Remember You*.

In addition to my hit, I also sang a duet with Alma. She was renowned for the extravagance of her gowns and she always impressed upon me the importance of dressing well on stage. Wanting to earn her approval, I'd taken extra care over my appearance that night and I thought we looked great together, I in my black suit and dickie-bow and she in one of her flamboyant be-sequinned creations. After the show she complimented me, saying I looked smart - and she was very proud of me. Praise indeed.

♪♫♪♫♪

I Remember You riveted itself into the number-one slot and remained there for an unbelievable eight weeks. What made it stand out so conspicuously to the recording industry was the fact it was all happening during the midsummer period, in what was traditionally known as the doldrums season for disc buying, yet it sold 367,000 copies in the first 5 days of release. That it happened without any substantial advance orders was just short of miraculous. Then, to cap it all off, at one point it was selling at the phenomenal rate of 102,000 copies a day, or an average 12,750 copies per hour or over 200 a minute, which made it one of Britain's fastest selling discs ever.

In fact, *I Remember You* was the first single to sell in excess of one million in Britain alone, and went on to the two million mark by the end of its first year. It remained in the charts for 28 weeks and its eight weeks at number one earned it a place in the *Guinness Book of Hit Records*. Even today it is rated as one of the most successful singles of all time.

Wow! No wonder I was left breathless. I obviously had high hopes for the record, but - get real! – not in my wildest expectations did I think I'd be regarded as an international pop star, let alone superstar. This was bordering on insanity. Oh, I know at the recording session I'd said I hoped for a number one - but then I'd always say that about each of my recordings. It didn't mean I believed it.

Despite the frantic search for the biggie, I had all the while considered it merely as the means to an end. Even now, in the wake of all that was happening, my purpose had not changed. I sought only to achieve success as an all-round entertainer, and the record was merely the key to open doors to the world's top venues, where I could prove my worth. I had never intended to become a pop star. Chart success on the scale that had been thrust upon me had just been a pipe dream and hadn't really come into the reckoning.

While I was certainly flattered by all the media attention and public adulation, I was also very afraid of losing my personal freedom. I love being with people and naturally seek out company - I am, by nature, an extremely gregarious person. However, I need my own space and liberty to go where I want, be with whom I want, do what I want and just be myself without having to answer to the ever intruding eyes of the camera or the prying pen of the journalist. Now, like it or not, here they were, stalking my every movement. Why, only a matter of a few weeks ago, nobody really cared a jot what I'd had for breakfast, what my favourite colour was or what was my opinion on world affairs. Now suddenly I was expected to make earth-shattering comments and put forward statements that would hit the headlines the following day. The fan magazines were obsessed with whether I enjoyed kangaroo-tail soup, what my ideal woman would be like, and what were my secrets to health, wealth and happiness. My only escape from all this was to hide away - a prisoner of my own success.

Of course, this was certainly not my first brush with fame. In Australia, I'd become somewhat accustomed to being a celebrity, having been in showbiz from an early age, and I'd always been able to handle the situation by keeping my private life separate from my public persona. But back home there had been an easy acceptance of me as a familiar personality. People would greet me with a friendly smile and a 'G'day mate'. Rarely had I felt hounded like this, and if ever the pressures did weigh on me, there was always the vast emptiness of the great outdoors to escape to, or the protective haven of home and family where I was always accepted as being myself.

Peter warned me to be wary, now I was in such high profile, that all sorts of people would suddenly crawl out of the woodwork to hunt me down. Some would be genuine, while others would just be out to make out of me what they could, and some possibly would come with downright evil intent.

So now my major concern was all the new people I was meeting. Must I treat them all with suspicion? Which of them would be friends? Did they want me for myself or did they just want to bask in my limelight? Was I just someone to be seen to rub shoulders with, or did they really want to get to know the real me?

I expected my long-standing friends to accept me just as they always had, but I was noticing that even some of them were beginning to alter the way they treated me. I suppose they were wondering how I would behave towards them now, and whether I'd become too high and mighty. I realised it was difficult for them, but it was even more difficult for me. I remembered my father's words, not to let success change me, yet no matter how much I wanted to remain the same, I was discovering it was impossible when close friends were changing their attitude to me. Already I was starting to wonder if fame as the price of success was too great a cost to bear.

In my chase for professional recognition, I'd spawned a monster and it was this ogre that threatened now to take control of my entire being. I hadn't seen myself as a pop idol, yet suddenly that was just what I was. My picture was in every newspaper and magazine, my voice played out continually over the airwaves and everywhere I went reporters, photographers and a growing army of fans pursued me. In the frenzied fever of those hectic days, there was no chance to stop and question whether this was what I really wanted. I'd been hauled firmly onto a

Make With the Eyes and Teeth

bandwagon, the brakes were off and it was hurtling into the future, propelling me in a direction I would not necessarily have chosen to go. There was no turning back now; for better or for worse, I would have to roll with the flow, wherever it may lead.

I Remember You catapulted me to stardom and crowds began to follow me wherever I went. Here I had just stepped out for a moment and hundreds of people appeared from nowhere. Can you spot me in the middle of this mêlée? (Answer on page 183.)

- 17 -

A Royal Flush

It was just like being stalled at the traffic lights after they have turned green. The barriers I had struggled against for so long were down and it was go - go - go! But there, looming large in the engagement book covering the months of December 1962 to March 1963, were the words "Mother Goose - pantomime, the Alexandra Theatre". Peter jabbed his finger against the entry, as if to point out the obvious and asked:

"What should we do about this?"

Preceding all this overnight fame, I'd been contracted to appear in Derek Salberg's pantomime in Birmingham. Only a few short weeks ago, I'd blessed my good fortune, seeing it as a guarantee of bread and butter for the winter. Yes, I did enjoy playing pantomime, but right now? Spend three months prancing about the stage playing Colin Goose to crowds of yelling school kids when I could be jet-setting around the world parading my new star status before a wide, cosmopolitan audience? That would indeed be acting the goose, wouldn't it?

"It's a shame I know, but what can we do about it?" I countered.

Peter took a deep breath and started hesitantly "Well..."

I didn't need Peter to tell me there were ways and means of getting out of it. We could simply cancel the booking and let them sue me for breach of contract. The sudden and dramatic change in my circumstances would be ample justification. Offers were now arriving with bids of megabucks which read to me like telephone numbers and the extra money would more than compensate for any damages I would have to pay. However, my conscience was troubled and I was in a quandary. Those juicy offers were mouth-wateringly tempting and I thirsted after them, but it would mean descending to the level of the very cheats and rogues my father disapproved of. From far across the waves I could hear my dad advising "Wrong is wrong, son, and no amount of rationalisation will ever make it right" and I knew what I had to do.

"OK, I must see it through. I've signed a contract and I'll stick by it and prove my word is as good as my bond."

There was a sigh of relief from Peter and a smile of approval for my integrity. It was no easy decision. Still, I felt, as I was planning to be around for the long run, those tempting offers would just have to wait their turn.

A Royal Flush

However, the pantomime wasn't due to start until December, so when an offer came in for October, to tour with the prolific American hit-makers, the Everly Brothers and their co-star Ketty Lester, I jumped at the chance. Ketty had currently enjoyed a number-four hit with *Love Letters*, and the Everly's record of *Crying In The Rain* had been riding high in the charts earlier in the year. I've been an ardent admirer of the Everly's music ever since they first broke onto the scene in 1957 with *Bye Bye Love*. They have been an inspiration to me and a whole generation, so I was naturally thrilled and honoured to be working with them.

Ketty Lester joined me on the Everly Brothers' ill-fated 1962 tour.

Rehearsals were on the Saturday afternoon, at the Granada Theatre, East Ham, London, where the tour would open the next day, October 14th. The Everlys were due to rehearse after me, and I ran through my act, excited at the thought of watching from the wings. To my dismay, as soon as I'd finished, we were all cleared from the theatre by the company manager, Wally Stewart. While we were kicking our heels in the dressing rooms, we became aware of some sort of emergency occurring in the theatre and the whisper went round that Don Everly had collapsed on stage during a run-through of *Cathy's Clown*.

All we were told officially was that Don had been taken ill, suffering from a stomach upset, yet the word we heard was he'd overdosed on a drug and had been taken to hospital to have his stomach pumped. He discharged himself from hospital on the Sunday, October 14th, and we expected he'd make it for the opening night of the tour that same evening.

However, he'd not turned up before I went on stage to close the first half of the show, and at the last minute, I was asked to extend my spot to give Phil an extra breathing space. I was worried, though not for myself – I'd worked with the band before and suddenly adding an extra number wasn't too much of a problem. No, my concern was for Phil, facing the prospect of appearing solo. The moment I came to the wings for my false tabs, I shot an enquiring look at Ketty. She shook her head, but I'd already seen my answer in the lowering of her eyes. I went back out to sing my last song. The crowd's reaction was superb, yet I couldn't delight in it fully, for although I didn't let it show to the unsuspecting audience, my mind was with poor Phil.

My anxiety deepened throughout the interval, watching for Don's arrival, which was becoming less and less likely with every passing second. By the time Ketty came to open the second half, I was far too preoccupied to fully appreciate her performance. I stood in the wings beside Phil while he waited and he admitted to me he was scared stiff, this being the first time in all his 14 years as an entertainer he had made a solo appearance. I could sense how lost, lonely and totally disoriented he must feel and I admired his courage. Even as he waited, he held onto a forlorn hope his sick brother still might turn up. Ketty came off to a tremendous ovation and the time had now arrived for Phil to face his worst nightmare and walk the stage alone.

The audience gave him an enthusiastic welcome that he accepted with a timid smile as he launched into a somewhat strained performance of *Lucille*. He was unnerved, finding himself constantly slipping back into the harmonies, and it sounded very odd. He announced how sorry he was that Don wasn't there, admitting that he'd never appeared alone before but he would do his best. He had the audience's sympathy as he continued with other well-known Everly hits, but was obviously struggling. It was only when a member of the Everly Brothers Trio, Joey Paige, stepped forward to sing Don's lead parts that his confidence improved. He finished with *Bye Bye Love* and accepted the storming applause his valiant efforts had earned.

Throughout his act I could see Phil keep glancing to the side, expecting his brother suddenly to appear and rush onto the stage to rescue him from his ordeal. What we didn't know was that Don had collapsed again and had been rushed back into hospital. Eventually, unbeknown to Phil, Don returned to the States. Loyal to his fans, Phil made the brave and momentous decision to continue the tour alone. It seems strange and quite unprofessional that nobody informed Phil or us, the cast, what was going on, though I did hear that the company manager, Wally Stewart, was doing his best to cover up for fear of having to cancel the tour and refund all the money.

With no official explanation offered, rumours abounded. The press, like a pack of hounds with the scent of blood in their nostrils, sniffed out every avenue in search of a story. Wally Stewart had his time cut out in protecting Phil against the battery of reporters and photographers, so kept him out of their way, travelling with him in a separate limousine.

Thwarted in their efforts to get at Phil and having to provide copy for their papers, they had to find someone else newsworthy to hound. And they did. Me! With my huge Number One, I was big news myself and, with no one to shield me from them, I was easy prey. I was being badgered to death, as they sought to extract from me the low-down on the bitter break-up. They got nothing from me – even the little I knew I wouldn't betray – yet they didn't let up. From the moment I showed my face, either at the theatre or the front of the hotel or even getting into the coach, there they were. It became so bad I had to lock myself in my dressing room, only to emerge to go on stage.

In the interests of sanity and self-preservation, I protested long and hard to my management back in London. Eventually the Grades' office provided me with a 'bodyguard' in the diminutive shape of road-manager Charlie King – he who had produced the Stockton pantomime *Dick Whittington*. He duly arrived with a car for me, complete with chauffeur. Maybe not as impressive as the stretched limousine in which Phil rode, but nonetheless it was quite something to me as I had not travelled in such style before. I felt like royalty as I climbed into the back and sat in splendid isolation behind the uniformed chauffeur, while we zoomed off to follow at the tail of the procession behind the company coach.

I confess I did wallow in the new experience for a while, but it didn't take long for the novelty to wear off. After the first hour or so, conversation with Charlie dried up, and I sat in silence staring at the towns and villages as they sped by my window, following one another in suburban monotony. I found myself gazing at the company coach in front, watching the heads of the Vernons Girls on the back seat bobbing up and down, imagining them convulsed in laughter at the jokes of comedian Norman Collier. I was envious of them, missing the camaraderie. Worse, though, was the change in relationship between us. I began to notice a schism opening up between myself and the rest of the company. Once warm and friendly, they now seemed cool to my approaches. "Look at him," I could feel them thinking, "far too superior to associate with us."

I was fearful that morale was dropping dangerously low and the show, already teetering on the brink of disaster due to Don's absence, was likely to collapse totally if this went on. My seeking of self-protection had

I Remember Me

been misinterpreted by them as a bid for status and had aggravated the problem, so I reckoned it was up to me to put it right.

Anyway, I'd had enough of playing the big lah-de-dah in the isolation of my car and longed to return to the fold. If I was unhappy for myself, then I was also distraught to watch the increasing toll the strain and stress were exacting on Phil. I knew he'd also be a lot happier and far more relaxed if he could be tempted out of his exile and into contact with the rest of us. Yet try as I might to get to speak with him, I was prevented from doing so by Wally's ultra protective zeal.

Determined not to be beaten, I finally barged right past Wally's barricades and into Phil's dressing room. Phil greeted me in wide-eyed surprise. I put my plan to him, suggesting he would have a lot more fun if we travelled together with our support acts on the coach. To my relief, his careworn face lit up into a big broad grin at the idea, the first spark of animation he had shown since the tour had started. Between us, we worked on Wally to allow his charge to leave the car.

Everyone beamed their welcome to Phil the next day, as he climbed with me up the steps onto the coach. We sat on the back seat, laughing together at the sight of two chauffeur-driven cars, each carrying one of the road-managers, following behind while their stars rode in the coach. It appealed to our sense of humour - and it saved the show.

It's not my intention to go into the detailed reasons for Don Everly's withdrawal from the show – I've written it here as I knew it at the time. The drug Don was taking was one he had on prescription, to help him deal with the stress and exhaustion of overwork. There isn't, and never was, any question of the use of illegal substances.

♪♫♪♫♪

I've been through some pretty harrowing experiences in my long and varied career, but on Monday October 29th 1962 occurred one of the most testing ordeals my nervous system has ever faced.

When I came to Britain, it had been with the ambition to play the London Palladium and I'd given myself the undeclared target of three years in which to achieve it. With immaculate timing, just one week before the expiry of this self-imposed deadline, came the offer I'd been waiting for. But it wasn't just a performance on that famous stage, it was also to be televised live throughout the world and in the audience would be Her Majesty The Queen and the Duke of Edinburgh. Yes, this was my

A Royal Flush

first Royal Command Performance. It's so well etched on my memory, I relive the ordeal every time I think of it...

I see my guitar being set on its stand by the stagehands while I wait in the wings for my cue. I feel none of the usual butterflies - no, indeed, they've taken flight leaving a swarm of giant moths whirling inside me, while my throat feels constricted by a band of fear so tight I wonder how I will breathe, let alone sing. I try out a little cough and a quick, subdued burst of a yodel as I usually do, in order to check that it is still in working order and, ah, yes it is...

This is it. Compere Norman Vaughan has just announced my name, the audience has started applauding... but wait, don't be too anxious now... hold back until it has reached its crescendo. Now take a deep breath and fix the smile - I hope it looks more natural than the stupid grin it feels like - straighten up and stride forward to acknowledge the welcome from the crowd.

So far so good. The introductory music from the orchestra has covered my entrance - it sounds fantastic - and I have made centre stage. But what's this? My legs are starting to shake... oh dear, and there's the harmonica phrase to *I Remember You* cueing me to sing... I hear the sound of my own voice - ah, yes, thank goodness, it sounds as clear as a bell.

It can only get better now - it usually does... but not this time. My knees are beginning to knock - I hope no one can see my trousers quivering. Oh no, what now? The quaking is spreading all over my body... I can feel the edges of my mouth trembling and now even my eyes are starting to twitch. I'll try a blink to gain control - yes, it seems to have worked, but for how long?

At the end of the song I bow, then, over the applause I turn upstage, take a deep breath and try to regain my composure while I sling my guitar round my neck and welcome the prop of its familiarity. The lights dim and the spotlight irises down and focuses on the stool upon which I place my quivering bum. I start to strum my guitar in three quarter time for the 'til-ready intro of *He'll Have To Go* while saying "hello" to my audience. Now, as I ease into the song, the orchestral strings follow, right on cue. Yes! The quaking in my legs has subsided. What a relief.

But - oh no - the tremor has transferred itself to my voice and with such a quiet and tender song, it accentuates every nuance of my singing - my vibrato control is definitely suspect. And now look, the TV cameras are coming in for a close-up... still, maybe nobody will

I Remember Me

notice. Anyhow the song is nearing the end... there - I've reached the last stanza "...he'll have to go". I finish. Lights blackout.

On the applause they snap back up to a full up finish as I go straightaway into the bright and happy showstopper *She Taught Me To Yodel*.

Somehow or other, I survived these three songs and I even remembered the all-important bow to the Royal Box before I made my escape. I felt certain the entire world must have been amused by my nervous twitches. But no, I was assured that none of it was obvious to anyone watching on TV, or to the audience. Just as well. In fact, Peter said I appeared calmly confident and as cool as a cucumber. I was further comforted to discover that most of my fellow artists felt the same that night, even the most experienced of performers, so I wasn't the freak I feared myself to be.

Standing in line to meet Her Majesty Queen Elizabeth II after a Royal Command Performance at the London Palladium.

A Royal Flush

Be that as it may it was not the end of the night's ordeals. Horrendous as it had been on stage, it was as nothing compared with standing in line waiting to be introduced to Her Majesty. How come I was feeling like a prisoner approaching the gallows, when it all seemed so natural for the rest? First in line was comic veteran Bob Hope confiding a quip, then Eartha Kitt who seemed to purr like a contented kitten. Next, Sophie Tucker took the Queen's hand and curtsied beautifully. Now a shared joke with Royal favourite Harry Secombe and then Cliff Richard, who seemed to converse with ease. She moved on, to The Shadows, Johnny Dankworth and his wife Cleo Laine, Edmundo Ross, Andy Stewart, Dickie Henderson, Eric Sykes, Mike and Bernie Winters... If only I'd been nearer the front, I thought, so there would be less time for these butterflies to eat me alive.

Admittedly this was my first occasion and hope I may be forgiven for standing there gawking as the Queen stated how she had enjoyed my performance and commented that it was nice to hear yodelling - to which I think I answered "Yes" or something equally stimulating. My conversation did improve somewhat in later Commands - well slightly anyway.

♪♫♪♫♪

Thank goodness Her Majesty approved of my yodel, for after years of labouring under Peter Gormley's edict of 'strictly no yodelling', the Great British Public was being exposed to the full Ifield yodel - and they loved it.

It's ironic, really, that despite his edict, it was Peter himself who'd suggested to me the very song that had brought me to public acclaim, and yet to trigger its success I'd slipped in the falsetto he had so adamantly forbidden. However, the public latched onto my 'little falsetto' in a big way. For its time, when the pop music of the fifties was sounding dated and the new decade had yet to find its own sound, it was the 'something different' which people yearned for - and soon imitations of my 'I Remember You-ooo' were reverberating off bathroom tiles all over the country.

The big question now was what would be the follow-up? I certainly didn't want to produce the carbon copy sound-alike so prevalent in those days. The answer seemed obvious to Norrie Paramor, for he thought it time the 'little falsetto' turned into a full-scale yodel.

Despite Norrie's confidence, I worried that Peter would be proved right and I would be branded as a yodeller, with a hard fight on my hands

I Remember Me

to prove my versatility. However, the greater danger was that after such a huge hit I'd be relegated instead to a 'one hit wonder' and fade without trace, just when everything was opening up for me. I needed another big hit and, if Norrie was sure the public were ready for my yodel, then perhaps that's what it should be. We recorded *She Taught Me How To Yodel*, but I fought shy of issuing it as an 'A' side. I really didn't want it to feature quite so prominently.

So the big problem now was to choose the right song for the top side. I wasn't left to tackle it alone, because it seems that everyone I knew, from Cliff and the Shadows down to the cleaners, was searching for me. They came up with many worthwhile possibilities, but it was singer Ronnie Carroll's suggestion that proved to be the winner. Ronnie had overheard me singing it to myself in a dressing room while waiting to appear on a TV show called *Thank Your Lucky Stars* and he thought I should record it. It was *Lovesick Blues*, the old Hank Williams song I always used to enjoy performing in Australia.

So there it was - the answer was under my nose all the time. It was ideal - just what we were looking for to develop and build on the falsetto sound from *I Remember You*, while at the same time producing a complete contrast. We wanted something different in both style and tempo and we certainly got it in Norrie's arrangement, which incorporated the latest dance craze, the Twist, with a brass ensemble.

I didn't dare believe it myself, but it seems the world was waiting eagerly for the follow-up to *I Remember You*. When it was released it had clocked up 200,000 in advance orders - the highest advance figure ever claimed by EMI for any British artist apart from Cliff Richard. Everyone was telling me that with advances like that it was a sure-fire chart topper, but I had learnt not to bank on anything in this business, for experience had shown me that even stone-cold certainties can come to nothing. Luckily, I was wrong and they were right, for on November 8th, 1962 *Lovesick Blues* became my second chart topper, making it two No 1's in succession - a rare feat indeed.

Norrie was right, too, about the public's awakened appetite for the yodel. Since my performance of *She Taught Me How To Yodel* in front of millions of viewers on the Royal Command, requests for it had been coming through in a rush to radio programmes and record shops. With such demand, the record buying public were not to be confounded by my efforts to keep it down and *She Taught Me How To Yodel* succeeded in becoming a double 'A', entering the charts in its own right.

A Royal Flush

There was no way anyone could expect *Lovesick Blues* to stay on top as long as *I Remember You*, especially as that first record was still selling well enough to keep it in the charts. Yet it stayed at number one for 5 weeks, an eminently respectable attainment and it became my second million-seller and gold disc.

At least one thing was sure - I was not to be consigned to the bin as a one-hit-wonder. I'd spent half of the last six months at the top of the charts, and despite being a 'nobody' at the beginning of the year, my name went down in the record books for 1962 alongside those of Cliff Richard and Elvis Presley.

The monetary rewards of my new-found fame were soon filtering through to my bank and the balance was now well in the black. At long last, I could wave goodbye to moth-eaten carpets, threadbare furnishings and the exorbitant rent of my upstairs flat in Blandford Street. I gathered together all of my possessions - my guitar, a wardrobe of clothes, and a marble horse's head given to me by Ron Grainer - and bundled them down the stairs and into the back of the brand new Ford Capri waiting for me in the street.

It looked sleek and sporty but was a selfish car. Good for just one companion with its comfortable bucket seats in the front, while discouraging a crowd with what was described as an occasional seat in the rear - hard on the bum and harder on the head, unless you bent double. I got into the driver's seat and forged my way through the Edgeware Road traffic towards Maida Vale, turned into Hamilton Terrace and drew up outside my new apartment. It had previously belonged to Russ Conway and when I learned he was looking to sell the place, I had viewed it, bowed to temptation and bought it before he could change his mind.

I opened the door and walked in. Pacing along the hallway, I poked my nose into each room as I passed: one bedroom, another bedroom and yet another, a kitchen bristling with all the latest appliances and my very own bathroom. Finally, I flung open the last door and the lounge spread out before me. A flood of daylight streamed in through the double French doors and I strode across to open them, letting in a rush of wintry air from the small garden.

Yes, it was November, the month of my 25th birthday and it was a good job I now had a comfortable retreat, because life was rapidly becoming even more hectic. For a start, I now had to find a follow-up to two number-one successes. Norrie had lined up three sessions at Abbey Road studios: November 14th produced *Confessin'* - my updated country-style version, November 20th produced *The Wayward Wind*, while

I Remember Me

November 27th produced a ballad called *Be Nobody's Darling But Mine*. This song, attributed to Jimmy Davis, former honky-tonk singer and latterly Governor of Louisiana, was actually acquired by Davis from an impoverished hillbilly named Bill Nettles, a prisoner brought to justice during Davis's days as a criminal court clerk.

On the evening of that last session, I returned home exhausted yet elated with the results of the day's work. I had just flopped into the all-embracing comfort of my armchair, when the insistent ringing of the telephone bell jangled into my tranquillity. Cursing at it, I went to answer.

My ears pricked up immediately at the sound of familiar accents on the line - voices from back home. One was that of Helen De Paul, the vivacious sister of the famed Flying De Pauls who were a highly successful acrobatic high-wire act and well established on the European theatrical circuit; the other was that of her young daughter, Patsy Ann Noble.

No sooner had I written down the address than I was off to visit them somewhere in Highgate. As I drove, exhaustion was forgotten, vitality flooded through my body and I could hardly contain my excitement. For so long now, my head had been spinning with the whirl of events happening around me, but just the sight of their familiar faces would bring this mad merry-go-round momentarily to a halt. I guess they represented a lifeline to the gentler reality of the life that I had left behind.

I rang the doorbell and waited. The door opened just wide enough for me to catch a glimpse of Helen... then all at once the quiet of the street exploded into shouts and screams of delight. I squeezed her in an embrace which almost took the breath from her, until she broke free and said, "You didn't expect to see us over here, did you Frank?"

Patsy Ann moved forward and before I knew it I was lifting her off her feet and spinning her round in circles. Then I held her at arms-length and went to speak but nothing came out - I hardly recognised the dark-haired beauty before me until she offered me her familiar smile, and I gasped, "Patsy! Look at you now... my, how you've grown!"

It was hard to credit that this pretty teenager was the same girl who had adopted me as her 'Uncle Frank', when she was just a cute little kid. For Patsy was the daughter of comedian Buster Noble, a close friend of mine, and Helen was his wife.

Buster and I used to appear together in Australian Country Music shows, where, far from just singing, I'd take part in comedy sketches. I'd spend many happy hours with them at their home in Marrickville, a suburb of Sydney, rehearsing these sketches, while Buster patiently coached me in the stagecraft and timing needed. Indeed, it was from him I learned the skills that have proved to be such a wonderful grounding for the pantomime roles I have played over the years.

Fellow Australian and friend from back home, Patsy Ann Noble, helps me to celebrate my 25th birthday.

As the memories of individual sketches came flooding back, Helen and I simply had to relive them, there and then. We couldn't help it. We took it in turns, egging each other on, until we both collapsed, overcome with laughter.

Patsy was too young back then to appear with us and could only watch awe-struck from the wings. "Maybe I was too little to join in," she said "but it was while I was watching you I vowed that come rain or hailstones, I would one day be a big star myself."

I Remember Me

"And from what I hear, you're already well underway," I told her. Indeed it was true, for I'd had many glowing reports of her successful appearances from my family. "Is that why you're here?"

"Yes. I thought I'd follow your example - since you've made it, then maybe I can too."

I looked into her glowing face, fresh with a youthful beauty rapidly ripening into maturity. In her eyes, I was no longer Uncle Frank; I was the sophisticated, successful, self-confident star she'd travelled half a world to emulate.

"I'm sure you will, Patsy, I'm sure you will," I said, giving her a hug.

Then, although it was a wrench to leave, I had to go. As it did all too frequently these days, time - or the lack of it - was depriving me of the company of the ones I loved. The merry-go-round that was my life allowed little time for respite. In fact, after hacking around the country with Phil Everly, I'd hardly had time to be reacquainted with my own pillow at home before I was zooming up and down the country again, this time headlining my own major tour.

- 18 -

LONESOME NUMBER ONE

I'd already changed out of my opening costume into my dressing gown and had settled onto the settee to await my next cue. This was the third time I'd played the Liverpool Empire but, before, I'd been relegated along with the also-rans to the meagrely furnished, shared dressing rooms on the top floor, rattling precariously up and down by means of an elderly wire cage lift. Now I was located at stage level, lording over a private dressing room and entertaining area, all by myself. I was just beginning to relax when the doorman came politely tapping at my door.

"Yes?"

"There's a gentleman at the stage-door wanting to see you, Mr. Ifield."

Another privilege of top-of-the-bill status was the protection from visitors - unwanted or otherwise. I was intrigued to know just who this gentleman was who warranted this interruption.

"Did he say who he was or what he wanted?" I asked.

"His name is Mr. Epstein and I thought you'd know him. He's smartly dressed, like a business man, and looks important."

As I had plenty of time before my next stage call, I thought I might as well see him. "You'd better show him in then."

He introduced himself as Brian Epstein, manager of a new pop group. "Ah, so that's it," I thought.

I might not have been at the top very long, but I'd already been pursued by persistent managers soliciting my influence on behalf of their protégés. I did try to be patient with them, for after all it wasn't too long ago that Peter and I had been doing precisely the same thing. Anyway, I found myself more readily disposed towards this man since I recognised in him something of the same approach we had used. He was well dressed, deferential and softened his perseverance with politeness.

"I'm sorry for taking up your time," he said humbly. "Perhaps you'd prefer if I came back later, after the show?"

I'd already made arrangements for a candlelight dinner for two that night and nothing was going to interrupt that. Anyhow, since he'd got this far, I was anxious to get the matter out of the way right now.

"No it's alright. Come inside. I'm not required on stage for some time yet, so have a seat," I said, pointing to the comfortable settee I'd just vacated.

I Remember Me

He did as I bid. "Would you have time to listen to a copy of my group's new record, *Love Me Do*?" he asked. "It's not long been out and it's proving to be a big seller."

"Yes sure," I sighed. I went to my record player and turned it on, thinking I was in for yet another of those boring demo discs.

But no. The sound that filled my dressing room was fresh, vibrant and full of enthusiasm. Surprisingly, it wasn't too dissimilar from my own style, for there were the mouth-organ phrases and the falsetto vocal breaks. I, too, had tried to avoid an overly polished sound on my own singles, but what I heard here had the essence of that same raw excitement I'd admired in Bruce Channel. I was highly impressed, though I tried not to sound over-enthusiastic.

"It's certainly catchy and has a lot of drive."

He persuaded me to play it through again and while I listened he handed me some publicity photos. 'The Beatles' they announced and my quick glance revealed four smartly dressed, tousle-haired lads, and I could see they would create quite an impact with the young girls.

The second hearing of the song only reinforced my first impression and I said so.

"I'm pleased you like it, Frank," he said.

Now he came to the nitty-gritty of his visit. "Would you consider using them on your next tour? The lads need some stage experience outside of the Liverpool club scene - somewhere they're not already known."

I knew immediately what he meant. It was important to them in the same way it had been for me to work outside of my accepted territory before chancing my arm in England. As top of the bill, I did have the power to make recommendations for certain artists as my support acts. I was confident that my recommendation would be acted upon, yet rather less confident in making it. After all, I hadn't actually seen the Beatles perform. However, I knew I'd heard something really special just now and was prepared to take the risk.

"All right. I'll phone in a moment and have a word with my promoter Arthur Howes, but he may well have already booked all the supporting acts, so I think maybe you should follow up and make an approach yourself." I gave him Arthur's telephone number.

"Thank you very much indeed. I'll attend to that immediately. I'm most grateful to you, Frank, for sparing time to listen - and for your help." With that, we shook hands and he took his leave.

I couldn't help but ponder over what had just passed. For a start, why he was so keen to have the group appear on my show? My shows and my music tended to appeal to a much wider age range than they were aiming for, yet on the other hand I was currently 'top of the pops' and gaining number-one hits, which had put me into prominence in the pop scene. Indeed, Arthur Howes' shows were pop concert oriented one-night stands, just the type of show that generally attracted a young audience, and therefore the kind of exposure this new group needed. Indeed I could anticipate the attraction the Beatles would have to the teenage members of my audiences. Yes, I convinced myself, I'd done the right thing. Either way, it was going to be an interesting experiment.

I had been right in supposing that all the support acts had been fixed, but as a result of my enthusiastic recommendation Arthur Howes booked the Beatles to appear on my show on December 2nd 1962 at the Embassy Cinema in his home territory of Peterborough. He arranged for the group to be given a ten-minute spot on each of the two houses that night, so he could appraise them for himself. They must have considered my show to be a big step in the right direction, or at least Brian had persuaded them this was so, because I understood they had to miss their show at the Cavern Club and they were to get no fee, other than expenses.

I arrived early at Peterborough. That morning, I'd been recording in London for the first of my 15-minute radio shows for Radio Luxembourg with the Ted Taylor Four, so I drove myself there. I went directly to my dressing room to hang up my clothes and settle in for the evening. Then I went to make friends with the stage of the Embassy Cinema, while my travelling kettle came slowly to the boil.

I already had the tea brewing in the pot when the tour bus arrived and the theatre became filled with the excited chat of the new arrivals - my friends the Viscounts, the Breakaways, Julie Grant and our band, the Red Price Combo. But so far, no Beatles. There was no mistaking their arrival though. It was announced in no uncertain terms by the sound of their Scouse accents resonating throughout the building.

It was around the time of the half-hour call for curtain up when they came to my dressing room to say hello. I asked them in and offered them a cup of tea, but as I was busy getting ready for the opening of the first show, I had to leave them to help themselves. The number-one dressing room at the Embassy Cinema was not built to the same lavish scale as the Liverpool Empire. There weren't enough seats and neither did my catering run to enough cups to go round, so they had to fight over which of them were to squat on the floor and which were to have the first cuppas. Smiling to myself at the commotion going on behind me, I returned to the task of putting on my stage makeup.

Eventually, the clattering of crockery ceased and all went quiet. Through the mirror, I became aware of four pairs of eyes watching intently as I applied my eyeliner and pan-stick makeup. Brian had obviously given them instructions to observe closely and learn how things are done in the theatre and they weren't about to miss a thing. Before they left my room to get ready themselves, I let them borrow some makeup. Unfortunately, they hadn't been watching closely enough, for when they duly appeared, they looked more like a swarm of red cochineal beetles.

I watched from the wings. In many ways I envied these new groups who worked with their own integral band, while I was expected to perform after one rehearsal with differing bands, or the more subdued tones of a pit orchestra. However, I remember thinking their volume was far too high. Having worked with the Shadows on many occasions, I was aware the back-stage volume was always louder when the band's amplifiers were on stage, even so this was way and above what was needed. It was bound to lead to complaints.

Volume apart, they presented themselves well. They were lively, full of exuberance and as far as I was concerned their individual personal charm was wholly infectious. Unfortunately, they didn't manage to convey that charisma to the crowd, who watched in horror, greeting their efforts not with applause but with shouts and boos.

This hostile response really concerned me. For a start, my own act was to follow and I would have to work all the harder to get such an antagonistic audience to warm to me. Secondly, I knew there would be flak flying from the theatre management, on account of the Beatles' excessive volume and what would appear to them to be a poor performance. And inevitably that flak would be heading in my direction, the group having appeared on my recommendation.

Thank goodness my first fear was unfounded, as the reception I received was one of resounding acclaim. Obviously, conclusions were drawn at the time from the marked contrast, but it's not a fair comparison at all. After all, the audience had come to see me and knew what to expect, but the Beatles' music coming out of the blue must have been a total shock to them. For historical interest, I quote an extract from columnist Lyndon Whittaker who reported in his review entitled, 'I'll Remember Frank Ifield'.

The 'exciting Beatles' rock group quite frankly failed to excite me. The drummer apparently thought that his job was to lead, not to provide rhythm. He made far too much noise and their final number, 'Twist and Shout', sounded as if everyone was trying to make more noise than the others. In a more mellow mood, their 'A Taste of Honey' was much better and 'Love Me Do' was tolerable.

There was no denying that the group had made an impact, albeit unfavourable, and the performance in Peterborough was destined to become an integral part of the Beatles legend. However, when the act "died" so ignominiously on that night in December 1962, who could have possibly predicted that these unaffected young lads were the chosen ones to spearhead a whole new wave of international British music? I certainly did not. Yet despite the reaction to them, I held onto my conviction that the Beatles were heading for great things and I wasn't ashamed of sticking my neck out for them. Thankfully, Arthur Howes spotted the talent I had seen and he booked them to continue for some remaining dates on my tour.

Apart from that traumatic first night, I recall little of the Beatles in following shows. I was living under such pressure that I needed to concentrate my energies on my own performances and, to me at that time, they were just another bunch of young hopefuls who showed great promise.

However, the Peterborough episode and my part in it, apparently made a lasting impression on the Beatles. What I didn't know then was that my *I Remember You* already featured in their repertoire and, going about their regular gigs, they often clashed with other groups on the bill over who was to perform this guaranteed showstopper. Shortly after Peterborough, when they made their last trip to the Star Club in Hamburg, Germany, the show was captured on a portable tape recorder. Many years later when that tape was released, there was *I Remember You* with Paul McCartney imitating my falsetto style and John Lennon raucously playing the mouth harp figures.

I also discovered later that, on their first date, Ringo Starr took Maureen Cox to the Liverpool Empire to see my show. I'm pleased to have acted as Cupid.

♪♫♪♫♪

I Remember Me

While the Beatles fled back home to Liverpool there was no respite for me. I was straight into rehearsals for the pantomime *Mother Goose*, which had been the subject of such heart-searching earlier in the year. Not only was I reconciled to it, I was genuinely looking forward to it. After all the exhausting touring, three months in one place held definite appeal, while the show itself promised to be first-class and a barrel of laughs into the bargain.

It starred Oscar-winning comedy actress, Beryl Reid, who played her then famous Black Country TV character, Marlene, as Mother Goose's maid, whilst Jack Trip played Dame in the title role. Also featured, as the broker's men, were the Dallas Boys – a well-known vocal group from Jack Good's TV series *Six-five Special* - comedian Ted Rogers took the part of Simple Simon and finally, yours truly played the role of Colin Goose.

Pantomimes are notoriously hard work and this one was no exception, as we had to perform at least two, three-hour shows per day and my role, extended in view of my star status, meant more time on stage, with little chance to rest. But I didn't mind. I was in my element - carte blanche to fool around both on and off stage, safe in the surroundings of a large and happy company.

The five Dallas Boys - Stan, Leon, Bob, Joe and Nicky - along with Ted and myself soon became known as The Magnificent Seven and didn't we make an inseparable team? We soon earned a reputation as a bunch of reprobates, creating mayhem both on and off stage.

The show featured a Scottish scene in which we all appeared wearing kilts and one night we made our stage entrance dressed... well, how shall I put it... how about 'authentically'? That is to say, if we were asked if anything was worn beneath the kilt, we could honestly reply in the words of Andy Stewart, "No, it's all in good working order."

With high kicks we launched into a Can-Can style routine which quickly had the females in the front stalls dissolving into fits of convulsive giggling. Nightly from then on the front rows would be filled with fans waiting with bated breath for the chance of seeing our unique Scottish Can-Can again.

That's pantomime for you. I was happy and secure in my role within it, but my role in the outside world was a different matter.

♪♫♪♫♪

The winter of 1962/63 was one of the coldest on record and the snow stayed so long on the ground it turned black. But this didn't deter me from driving all the way back to London to spend Christmas Day with my girlfriend Dolly. Dolly had been at my side sharing with me the flowering of my new success and yet that very success had now brought about a pressure of work that was inevitably driving us apart. Being in pantomime did not mean the trappings of my new star role had ceased. I was kept busy most workaday mornings with radio and newspaper interviews and on Sundays there were various charity shows and Sunday concerts in far flung places, while she was living in London, having found full-time employment as a Bunny Girl in Hugh Heffner's Playboy Club.

Appearing in the pantomime Mother Goose at the Birmingham Alexander theatre put my burgeoning career on hold for a few weeks at the beginning of 1963.

I endeavoured to see as much of her as I could, and so too did the many avid readers of Playboy magazine where she displayed her naked exquisiteness in the centrefold as 'Playmate of the Month'. However, it was becoming increasingly evident that our relationship could not develop under these conditions, so when she was offered the chance to work in America, I didn't stand in her way. She went off to pursue her dream, while I stayed on, pursuing mine.

A year or so later, she came to see me when I was working in Los Angeles, still emanating that soft, feminine appeal I found so enticing. It was here I learned she had met and married American comedian Dick Martin of *Rowan and Martin's Laugh-In* fame. So it was, with wistful

I Remember Me

smiles, we went our separate ways once more, remembering the good and the splendour of all we meant to each other. We parted for the last time wishing one another love.

♪♫♪♫♪

Success had squeezed Dolly out of my life, yet this was only one symptom of a personal lifestyle that was changing radically. It's true, I didn't have to struggle any more and it felt good not having to doss down in dirty digs. Yet by the same token, my deluxe suite at the Albany Hotel in Birmingham was beginning to feel more like Brixton prison. I was finding it impossible to get out.

If I wanted to go for a walk or simply browse around the shops, I would be descended upon by hordes of autograph hunters as soon as I stepped foot outside the hotel, and would have to give up the idea and retreat back to my room. Even the hotel staff were becoming fed up with the constant chanting of the crowds of fans lingering outside the doors and breaking into the lobby. My typically Sagittarian nature demanded freedom and space, and so, with the liberty to wander in peace denied me, my private life was being made a hell. I would just spend my free time alone in my room in comfortable boredom, then would head straight for the theatre.

I needed the company of people I liked to be near, so I tried to persuade Ted Rogers to book into the Albany with me. He protested he simply couldn't afford it, so I went to great lengths to arrange with the management to allow him to stay at a special rate, so he couldn't refuse. Life brightened up no end after that. We would spend the mornings having fun, and often the Dallas Boys would call in, too. I guess they filled a void left by the absence of my brothers, and Ted especially offered companionship at a time when I was in desperate need of a mate I could trust. It was the start of a long friendship, and the beginning of a mutual admiration society that built up steadily between us over the years.

Even so, to maintain my sanity, there were times I felt I simply had to break away from the hotel. Ted thought he had the answer when he dressed me up in a balaclava, a large-brimmed hat and dark glasses, so I could go out without being mobbed. However, the disguise only made me more conspicuous than ever.

One day, I decided enough was enough. I would brave the hordes and the freezing weather - and all to buy Ted a birthday present. There was no way I could venture out alone, so I had to drag my minder, Fred, along with me, simmering with undisguised indignation at having been forced out of his cosy room for such a frivolous expedition. We entered a store where I chose the perfect gift and asked the assistant to wrap it. Clutching my purchase, I made my escape, with Fred's help, to the safety of the theatre, where he scuttled away thankfully to make a cup of tea and warm up again while I placed my surprise package on the dressing table and chuckled to myself.

When Ted arrived, I handed him the beautifully wrapped gift. He feigned a protest saying, "Oh, Frank, you really shouldn't have."

"I know I shouldn't," I said, trying to mask the grin that threatened to ruin the plot by breaking out all over my face. "Go on - open it."

So, he did. Then... wham! His face was priceless - stunned surprise, shock, and then repulsion, as he screwed his nose up in disgust. I exploded with laughter. He resisted the temptation to stuff the wrapping into my open mouth and instead held up at arm's length the most hideously garish pair of socks you ever saw - in flaming red and yellow plaid. But then, to my surprise, he put them on and went on stage, where he produced a huge laugh out of them. He was a game guy.

Ted and the boys were not put on this earth solely for my benefit, though, and I still had many hours on my own. Staring out of the window of my hotel room onto huddled figures squelching through the dirty-grey slush in the streets below, I would drift into a wistful dream of my home in Sydney, bathed in the heat and glorious sunshine of an Australian summer.

"This is my reward, is it?" I would muse, "for achieving fame and fortune here in Britain. All right, so it's a wonderful country with friendly people and the theatrical scene is marvellous - and if I were to leave, I would sorely miss it all." Yet, I have to confess that as I sat in solitary confinement in my luxury prison, I often found myself longing to return to my family and friends. The pressures were building up and, without Dolly, were becoming just too hard to bear on my own.

1962 had been the most successful and exciting year of my life and 1963 lay ahead, full of promise. Yet there were many times I became so disheartened I seriously did consider giving it all up to return home.

- 19 -

FLIGHT TO THE FUTURE

It is amazing what a brush of spring sunshine can do. As I emerged from pantomime into the real world, there it was, beaming down on me full of the promise of new beginnings. I rushed off from Birmingham, scattering the shades of depression as I went, and stepped out into the full blaze of what could only be described as a glittering future. I was on my way to America.

While I had been shivering in my ivory tower at the Albany, things had really been hotting up around me. For a start, there was a battle royal going on in the charts. I'd already chalked up two Number Ones in succession, two more than I'd expected and no one but Elvis had ever achieved the seemingly impossible hat trick. My new release, *The Wayward Wind*, had been chosen as the vehicle to attempt the dizzy ascent to a third Number One and, since the record had been released with advance orders of 300,000, it was in with a definite chance of making the impossible possible.

Nevertheless, it was nail-biting stuff as it raced up the charts in direct competition with the new upstarts from Liverpool, the Beatles, who seemed hell bent on keeping me from attaining the premier position. Helped no doubt by the national exposure on the shows they had done with me, the Beatles' *Love Me Do* had finally hit the Top Twenty and they had been booked by Arthur Howes to tour with Helen Shapiro. They were out there at that very moment, causing a storm over the entire country, with fans clamouring to buy their second release *Please Please Me*. Ironically, this song, according to John Lennon, was inspired by the old Bing Crosby song *Please* he'd heard me sing on stage.

Beatles or no, the fates were not through with me yet - this was still my time. On February 21st 1963 *The Wayward Wind* hit the summit and I made history. Yes, the Guinness book of records proclaimed that I had the honour to be the first British artist to have three consecutive number-one hits. Wow! Peter, Norrie and I were thrice blessed in scoring the much-coveted hat trick.

As for the Beatles, did they or did they not make the top? According to the *New Musical Express* (NME), yes they did - but they had to share it with me. Guinness, however, basing their statistics on the *Record Retailer* charts, register that no, they didn't. For three weeks I held onto the top, beating off their challenge by keeping them at number two. So was *Please Please Me* the Beatles first number one? It has remained ever more a disputed issue amongst Beatles' historians. Be that as it may, what isn't in dispute is that *The Wayward*

Flight To The Future

Wind did indeed beat off the Beatles' challenge and became my third successive number-one.

Offers of the kind I'd always dreamed of had been flooding in ever since *I Remember You* had flung me into the big time, enabling me to cherry pick the juiciest. However, there was one fruit which remained temptingly just out of reach and that was the land of the Big Apple – New York, the USA. To pluck it, I would need the help of that elusive commodity, a hit record in America.

Apart from Lonnie Donegan in 1956 and 1961, no other British solo vocalist had successfully penetrated the American Top Ten. If Cliff Richard, with his track record hadn't made it, then what chance did I have? Nevertheless, EMI decided to try. The Capitol record label, EMI's US subsidiary, had first refusal on all of its British output, so in the summer of 1962, they were offered the latest package, the hottest attraction being my *I Remember You*, then at number one in Britain. Capitol were not impressed. They half-heartedly released my record and turned the rest of the package down - a package that included the Beatles. Yes, the giant Capitol rejected the Beatles - an error of judgement on a par with Decca's now classic rejection of the group in Britain.

Their apathetic attitude appeared to be a kick in the teeth for my hopes of hitting it big in America, but Norrie Paramor refused to be put off. Dissatisfied with Capitol's promotion, he felt we would be far better off with a smaller, more active company and, indeed, this is just what he found in Vee-Jay Records. An unlikely choice on the face of it, since it was a renowned independent R&B label specialising almost exclusively in black American artists. However, Vee-Jay were looking to expand, and with an eagle eye on my British chart-busting success, they were willing to take a chance on me.

As a reward for this confidence, and as if to thumb its nose at Capitol and all the other big US record companies, *I Remember You* forged its way up the US charts through the teeth of the opposition to reach number 5 in October 1962. It was a great surprise to me, too, that I should succeed where others had failed. Close on its heels, Vee-Jay released an LP of my British recordings, *Meet Frank Ifield*, and by February 1963 this was also a resounding success.

In order to capitalise on the sales, I was summoned by the record company for a promotional tour of Stateside radio stations to launch my next single, *Lovesick Blues*. Any lingering thoughts of returning to Australia evaporated, as I shook off the shackles of Colin Goose and flew west, following my dream to the New World.

I Remember Me

♪♫♪♫♪

It was difficult to believe that only twelve short months ago, I'd been in the depths of despondency, my recording contract about to come to an end and Norrie having rejected the concept on which I had pinned my last hopes. Now, thanks to *I Remember You*, my life had been transformed. The press and the public love a story of overnight success, and they went overboard with mine. They were wrong, of course, for in my case 'overnight' was far from true. Half a lifetime it had been since I had stood on a makeshift stage in front of parents and friends at a small school concert in the bushland of Australia and pledged myself to a career as a performer. I had struggled and fought for it ever since.

It's perhaps fortunate we can't see the future, for we would be deprived of hope, ambition, anticipation, excitement, and all those magical, fantastical expectations tingling through me at that time in my life. Indeed, the prizes were to be huge. The world's biggest venues – the London Palladium, the Paris Olympia, Las Vegas and even the Grand Ole Opry, all those targets I'd set myself as lad back in Australia - would become my stage; I would receive honours by the score; I was to become an international star. On a personal front, I would have the opportunity to travel to places I'd always dreamed of seeing, meet many wonderful people, make true friends of artists who were my idols and, most important of all, find love, a wife and a family.

If we were granted the vision of a seer, we would be starved of the quirky element of surprise which adds so much spice to life. Little could I imagine the many extraordinary situations I would be plunged into. For a start, the seeds had already been sown for me to become involved at the grass roots of two of the major transformations of pop music – the birth of pirate radio in Britain and the Beatles' storming of America – both of which would be written into the history of that glorious decade of the sixties, and me with them

However, it is said there is no gain without pain. I had already had my fair share of that, and Fate would make sure there was yet more tragedy, trauma and misfortune in store for me to face. But on that February day in 1963, when the plane lifted me into the skies above London and onto my next big adventure, all I had eyes for were the rewards unfolding in front of me.

If you didn't find me in the picture on page 157, you can just spot the back of my head in the centre of the picture between the two men wearing suits and white shirt collars

- INDEX -

A

ABC TV (Australia), 101
   Barbecue, 101
   Make Ours Music, 101, 108
Alldiss, Barry, 131
Allen, Frank, 151
Ambrose, 136
Armstrong, Louis, 92
Ashton, Queenie, 74

B

Bandstand, 96, 110
BBC Radio
   Easy Beat, 130
   Saturday Club, 123, 130, 142
Beatles, 171–75, 180, 181, 182
Bennett, Cliff, and the Rebel Rousers, 151
Big Chief Little Wolf, 51–55
Bonnington's Bunkhouse Show, 72, 73, 74, 86
Bourke, Charlie, 142
Breakaways, 173
Brennan, John, 82
British TV
   Thank Your Lucky Stars, 123, 166

C

Campbell, Big Bill
   and his Rocky Mountaineers, 14
Caplan, Sid, 136
Carey, Rick and Thel, 59, 60
Carroll, Ronnie, 144, 166
Channel 7, 96
   Sunny Side Up, 96
Channel 9, 94
   Campfire Favourites, 94, 95
Channel, Bruce, 147, 151, 172
Coalston, Lofty, 94
Cochrane, Eddie, 92
Cogan, Alma, 154
Collier, Norman, 161
Connors, Lily, 59, 74
Conway, Russ, 167
Craven, Howard, 73
Crawford, Allan, 59, 60, 61, 62, 74, 128, 129

D

Dallas Boys, 176, 178
Dankworth, Johnny, 165
Davis, Sammy Jr, 92
Dawson, Peter, 14, 108
Dawson, Smoky, 43
Day, Margaret, 107
Day, Vera, 141
De Paul, Helen, 168
Dear, Terry, 63
DeGray, Slim, 79
Deltones, The, 96
Dennis, Col and Lorna, 86, 87, 121
Disley, Diz, 151
Dorsey, Gerry. *See* Humperdinck, Engelbert
Dunn, John, 30
Dusty, Slim, 43, 79

E

Eddy, Duane, 136
Edinburgh, Duke of, 163
Epstein, Brian, 171
Everly Brothers
   Don, 159, 160, 162
   Phil, 159, 160, 161, 162, 170

F

Faulkner, Chuck, 95
Ford, Clinton, 130
Ford, Emile, 125, 127
Formby, George, 125, 128
Foster, George, 74

G

Goddard, Laine, 109
Gollah, George, 110
Gordon, Lee, 92
Gormley, Peter, 103–10, 114–21, 130, 131, 132, 137, 138, 140, 142, 143, 145–47, 153, 156, 158, 164, 165, 166, 171, 180
Grade, Leslie, 119
Grainer, Rel, 128
Grainer, Ron, 127, 167
Grant, Julie, 173
Gussey, Jim, 101

H

Hall, Ben, 29, 30
Harris, Jet, 133
Hawkins, Johnny, 139, 140
Hazelwood, Lee, 136
Henderson, Brian, 96
Henderson, Dickie, 165
Heylen, Sid, 96
Hill, Vince, 130, 143
Holly, Buddy, 92
Hope, Bob, 165
Howe, Bob, 1
Howes, Arthur, 172, 173, 175, 180
Humperdinck, Engelbert, 143
Hurst, Nola, 72

I

Ifield Brothers, 110
Ifield, Colin (brother), 13, 14, 38, 39, 99, 110, 111
Ifield, David (brother), 14, 99, 100, 111
Ifield, Frank
  Ancestry, 25–31
  Army, National Service, 88–90
  Arrival in England after Comet flight, 117
  Australia's first TV music show, 94–96
  Beatles, Frank Ifield Show, Peterborough, 171–75
  Big Chief Little Wolf, touring with, 51–55
  Birth, 3
  Childhood in Dural, Australia, 33–40, 41–47
  Childhood in wartime England, 3–14
  Decision to leave Australia, 101–2
  Departure for England, 110–12
  Duane Eddy, tour, 136
  Emigration to Australia, 15–16, 18–24
  Emile Ford, tour, 125–27
  First love, 84–88
  First professional stage appearance, 57–58
  First radio show, *Australia's Amateur Hour*, 66–68
  First record, 74
  First recording session, 70–72
  First single in England, 122–23
  First stage appearance, Dural, 45–46
  I Remember You hits no. 1, 152–54
  I Remember You, first public performance, 151–52
  I Remember You, initial concept, 144
  Influence of Rock and Roll, 91
  Learning to yodel, 14, 41–44
  Move to Beecroft, Sydney, 49
  Pantomime
    Mother Goose, Birmingham, 179
  Peter Gormley becomes manager, 103–5
  Pirate Radio, Allan Crawford, 128–30
  Royal Command Performance, 1962, 162–65
  Stock car racing, 86–87
  Sydney Stadium Show, 92
  targets of ambition, 82
  Tough early days in England, 120–22
Ifield, grandfather Peppa, 26–31, 37, 41, 43, 44, 52, 82–83
Ifield, Hannah Muriel (mother), 3–7, 11, 13, 18, 21, 25, 39, 42–46, 49, 52, 53, 55, 65, 66, 70–73, 76, 79, 80, 82, 91, 94, 99–101, 103, 104, 107–12, 117, 118, 121, 140, 153–54
Ifield, Jim (brother), 4, 6, 26, 36, 40, 41, 44, 47, 99, 111
Ifield, John (ancestor), 31
Ifield, John (brother), 6–8, 26, 36, 39–40, 41, 44, 47, 50–52, 59, 88–90, 98–100, 110, 111, 140, 153
Ifield, Philip (brother), 37, 46, 99–100
Ifield, Richard Joseph (father), 4–6, 9–11, 12, 13, 15–16, 17, 18–19, 21–24, 25, 27, 31, 33–34, 36, 38, 41–44, 45, 47, 49, 54, 65, 68, 69–71, 73, 74, 75, 82, 83, 86, 92, 93, 99–100, 103–4, 110, 111, 140, 153, 154, 156, 158
Ifield, Robert (brother), 3, 11, 38–39, 44, 46, 99–100, 110, 111

J

Jarrett, Eddie, 119, 121, 123
Joye, Col, 96
Judd, Noel, 74

K

Kalang (Sydney showboat), 97
Kidd, Johnny, and the Pirates, 151
King, Charles, 135, 161
King, Kevin, 72
King, Ted, 131
Kingston, Bob, 128
Kirby, Kathy, 125, 130, 136
Kitt, Eartha, 165

L

Laine, Cleo, 165
Laws, John, 96, 153
Legarde Twins, Tom and Ted, 50, 51
Lennon, John, 175, 180
Lester, Ketty, 159, 160
Lindsay, Reg, 72, 73
Little, Jimmy, 72
Livesey, Bessie (grandmother), 4, 6, 10, 11, 13, 15, 18, 20, 25, 37, 43–45, 45, 99, 100, 108, 111, 140, 153
Livesey, William (grandfather), 11
Lloyd, Jimmy, 125
Luciani, Alf, 95

M

Mack, Tommy, 57
Marvin, Hank, 133, 143
Mason, Malcolm, 76, 80
Matthews, Brian, 130
McCartney, Paul, 175
McClinton, Delbert, 151
McGregor, John (great grandfather), 11–13, 25
McKean, Sisters, 74
McNamara, Daphne, 68, 79
McNamara, Tim, 57, 68, 72
Mehan, Tony, 133
Meredith, Freddie, 79
Mersey, Gus, 74
Miller, Bob, 130
Mills, Gordon, 142
Mitchell, Guy, 50, 119, 120
Monro, Matt, 144
Morton, Tex, 43

N

Nelson, Constable Samuel (g.g.grandfather), 29, 30
Nichols, Nev, 72
Noble, Buster, 79, 168, 169
Noble, Patsy Ann, 168, 170

O

O'Connor, Des, 136
Orbison, Roy, 130

P

Pantomime
    Dick Whittington, 132–36
Paramor, Norrie, 118–19, 145–50, 131, 132, 143, 144, 150, 153, 165, 166, 168, 180, 181, 182
Payne, George, 79
Piercy, Denny, 130
Pitch, Harry, 148, 150
Platt, Ken, 135
Platters, 92
Power, Duffy, 142
Presley, Elvis, 167, 180
Price, Red, 173

Q

Queen Elizabeth II, 163, 165
Quigg, Ted, 79

R

Radio 2BG
    Australia's Amateur Hour, 63, 64, 65, 66, 68, 71, 74, 97
Radio 2GB, 63, 66, 72
Radio 2KA, 86
    Voice Of The Mountains, 86
Radio 2KY, 87
Radio 2SM, 72, 74, 80, 81, 82, 93
    On the Trail, 72, 74
Radio 2UE, 73, 81
    Sundown Singsong, 73, 86
    Vincent's Youth Parade, 73, 81, 86
Randall, Alan, 125, 136
Reddy, Helen, 96
Reddy, Max, 96
Reid, Beryl, 176
Richard, Cliff, 118, 131, 132, 134, 138, 143, 146, 152, 165, 166, 167, 181
Rodgers, Jimmie, 43, 92
Rogers, Ted, 176, 178
Ross, Edmundo, 165

S

Scott, Frank, 73
Scott, Gordon, 95
Secombe, Harry, 165
Shadows, 118, 131, 132, 133, 138, 143, 165, 166, 174
Shapiro, Helen, 180
Siggley, Ernie. *See* Williams, Ernie
Snow, Hank, 43, 52, 57, 71, 86
Starr, Ringo, 175
Steele, Tommy, 114, 116

Stewart, Andy, 165, 176
Stewart, Wally, 159, 160, 161
Sykes, Eric, 165

T

Tanner, Des, 73
Taylor, Ted, 173
Theale, Leonard, 74
Thomas, Al, 79
Tingwell, Charles, 73
Trip, Jack, 176
Tucker, Sophie, 165

V

Vaughan, Norman, 163
Vee Jay, 181
Vernons Girls, 161
Vincent, Gene, 92

Viscounts, 142, 173
Voight, Reon, 87

W

Walshe, Keith, 74
Webb, Graham, 93
Welch, Bruce, 133, 143
Whelan, Albert, 14
Whittle, Frank, 10
Williams, Buddy, 43
Williams, Cissy, 136
Williams, Ernie, 131
Williams, Hank, 43, 166
Williams, Neil, 74, 101, 136
Wills, Ron, 60, 61, 62, 64, 66, 70, 71
Winters, Bernie, 139, 165
Withers, Tony, 80, 81

For future publication...

I Remember Me, Too

FRANK IFIELD AUTOBIOGRAPHY
Volume 2
The Sixties and Beyond

If you remember **Frank Ifield** in the sixties, and wondered what happened next ...
If you remember the **Beatles, Cliff Richard, Pirate Radio, Roy Orbison, The London Palladium, Louis Armstrong**, and want to learn about them some gems you never knew ...
If you enjoy a good story splashed with humour, a tale of romance, heartbreak, heartache, tragedy and triumph ...

then this is the book for you!

Visit Frank's web site
www.frankifield.com
to contact Frank and catch up on his latest news and activities.
The site is packed with pictures, snippets, facts and memories.
Log onto the guest book and add your own contribution.

You've read the story, now hear the music

FRANK IFIELD SINGS COUNTRY AND CLASSICS

30 tracks recorded by Frank in Australia in the 1950s, digitally remastered from the original Regal Zonophone and Columbia recordings. Witness the true Country foundations to Frank's music.

Includes *Gipsy Heart, True* and other songs featured in the book, many of them never released since the original recording, all of them 'must-own' rarities.

EMI Gold 7243 5 41734 2 4

FRANK IFIELD - THE COMPLETE A-SIDES AND B-SIDES

A 3 CD box set of the 'A' and 'B' sides of all the singles recorded by Frank for EMI in the UK. As well as all the hits, re-live the hopes and disappointments that went into pre-*I Remember You* singles, such as *Lucky Devil, Gotta Getta Date, Tobacco Road* and *Alone Too Long*. This album has been specially compiled and released to coincide with the publication of this book. Available May 2005.

EMI Gold 7243 4 74544 2 4

A COWBOY'S LIFE IS GOOD ENOUGH FOR ME

A 4 CD box set of original pre-1955 recordings from various country artistes. The set includes two Frank Ifield tracks, *A Mother's Faith* and *There's a Love Knot in my Lariat* (the song Frank sang on *Australia's Amateur Hour* in 1952). There's also a selection of tracks by other artistes who people the book and who had an influence over Frank's early years, including Tim McNamara, Smoky Dawson, Hank Snow, Reg Lindsay, the Legarde Twins and Tex Morton

Jasmine JASBOX 13-4